The Art of Virtual LEGO Design

Design LEGO Models Using Studio 2.0

Vishnu Agarwal

Apress®

The Art of Virtual LEGO Design: Design LEGO Models Using Studio 2.0

Vishnu Agarwal
Bangalore, Karnataka, India

ISBN-13 (pbk): 978-1-4842-8776-7   ISBN-13 (electronic): 978-1-4842-8777-4
https://doi.org/10.1007/978-1-4842-8777-4

Managing Director, Apress Media LLC: Welmoed Spahr
Acquisitions Editor: Susan McDermott
Development Editor: James Markham
Coordinating Editor: Jessica Vakili

Distributed to the book trade worldwide by Springer Science+Business Media New York, 1 NY Plaza, New York, NY 10004. Phone 1-800-SPRINGER, fax (201) 348-4505, e-mail orders-ny@springer-sbm.com, or visit www.springeronline.com. Apress Media, LLC is a California LLC and the sole member (owner) is Springer Science + Business Media Finance Inc (SSBM Finance Inc). SSBM Finance Inc is a **Delaware** corporation.

For information on translations, please e-mail booktranslations@springernature.com; for reprint, paperback, or audio rights, please e-mail bookpermissions@springernature.com.

Apress titles may be purchased in bulk for academic, corporate, or promotional use. eBook versions and licenses are also available for most titles. For more information, reference our Print and eBook Bulk Sales web page at http://www.apress.com/bulk-sales.

Printed on acid-free paper

Table of Contents

About the Author

Vishnu Agarwal has years of experience in the field of STEAM Education using the LEGO Education platform. He is the founder of **ROBO-G**, a robotics and STEAM education service provider. Vishnu has successfully coached teams in the World Robot Olympiad and First LEGO League competitions. Many students and teachers alike have learned STEAM concepts from Vishnu's courses and coaching.

He has also presented a research paper on Teaching Programming and Computational Thinking to Elementary Level Children Using LEGO Robotics Education Kit at Technology for Education (T4E) at IIT, Bombay.

He is also the founder and LEGO artist at **Pick A Brick - Build Your Imagination**. He uses LEGO bricks to make people's imaginations come to life through custom models, workshops, and employee engagement activities. In other words, he 3D prints their thoughts using LEGO bricks.

He is the author of **"The Art of Virtual LEGO Design: Design LEGO Models Using Studio 2.0"** published by Apress, a Springer Nature company.

Introduction

Bricklink Studio 2.0 is completely free software that is widely used by LEGO designers to create LEGO models virtually before making them with real LEGO Bricks. You will have the freedom to build whatever you want using virtual LEGO bricks. As the Studio is integrated with the BrickLink catalog, it can do things like showing you what part colors are unavailable and let you keep track of part costs. Studio also makes it easy to turn a finished creation into a wanted list that you can use to order through BrickLink. You can also create professional building instructions for your model. To download the software you can visit `https://www.bricklink.com`. The studio 2.0 user interface is shown in Figure 1.

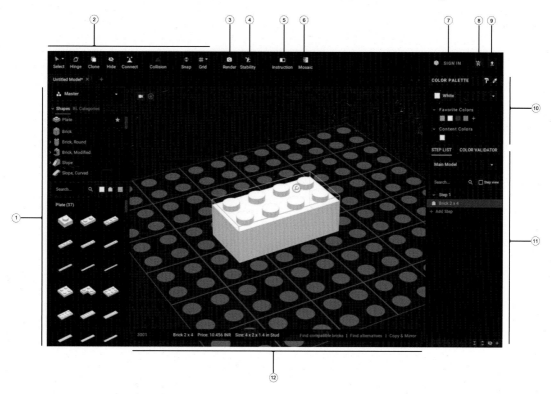

Figure 1. *Studio 2.0 user interface*

CHAPTER 1

Getting Started

In this chapter, you will learn how to start a new project, place and move a part, explore the basics of camera control options, and many other basic features.

Welcome Screen

When you launch the Studio the first time, the welcome window will appear on the screen, as shown in Figure 1-1. You can start a new project, open any existing Studio file, or import any existing models (Studio/LEGO Digital Designer/LDraw).

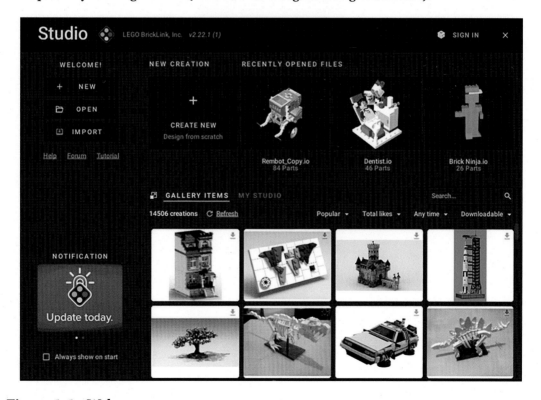

Figure 1-1. *Welcome screen*

V. Agarwal, *The Art of Virtual LEGO Design*, https://doi.org/10.1007/978-1-4842-8777-4_1

You can create an account on BrickLink and connect with the other users of Studio. You can also check a small tutorial on how to use the software.

There will be a recently opened file list. Also, you will get inspired by the gallery items where you will get models designed by Studio users around the world.

Starting a New Project

Click on **New** to start a new project, as shown in Figure 1-2. You can also create a new project through **File ➤ New**, as shown in Figure 1-3.

Figure 1-2. *New project option on welcome screen*

Figure 1-3. *Opening new project through file option*

Open an Existing Project

Click **Open** to open any existing project in your system on the welcome screen, as shown in Figure 1-4. You can also open an existing project through **File ➤ Open**, as shown in Figure 1-5.

Figure 1-4. *Open an existing project option on welcome screen*

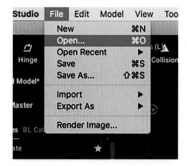

Figure 1-5. *Open an existing project through file option*

You can open your recent creations under **Recently Opened Files**, as shown in Figure 1-6.

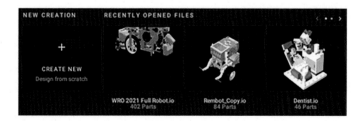

Figure 1-6. *Recently opened files*

Import a Model

You can import .io, .mo, .mpd, .lxf, .lxfml files by clicking **Import** on the welcome screen, as shown in Figure 1-7.

Figure 1-7. *Import a project option on welcome screen*

You can also import .io, .mo, .mpd, .lxf, .lxfml files, Official LEGO Sets, 3D Models and Mosaic through **File ➤ Import**, as shown in Figure 1-8.

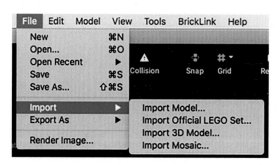

Figure 1-8. *Import a project through file option*

Studio Update

The Studio app will automatically check for available updates when you launch the Studio app. If there is any update available, you will see a pop-up to update, as shown in Figure 1-9. Simply click the "Update now" button to easily install it. If you do not see this pop-up, it means that you are already using the latest update, and no further action is needed.

Figure 1-9. *Studio update pop-up*

If you choose not to update Studio to the latest version then most of the key features such as basic building functions will not be affected even if you decide to stick with older versions. However, in-app login, uploading to Wanted List or My Studio will no longer be supported, and you will not be able to retrieve up-to-date catalog information.

Placing a Part

There are two ways to place the parts from the building palette to the build plate.

Left-click the part that you want to use, as shown in Figure 1-10. Then move the part toward the build plate and left-click again where you want to drop the part, as shown in Figure 1-11. As soon as you drop the part on the build plate, the part will be highlighted with a blue outline. In this method of placing the part after you drop the part on the build plate, the part will stick to the mouse pointer and start giving you a copy of the part, as shown in Figure 1-12. To get rid of this, you can right-click or press the ESC button.

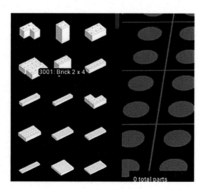

Figure 1-10. *Selecting the part*

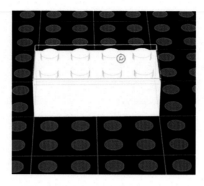

Figure 1-11. *Dropping the part*

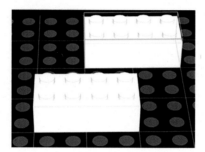

Figure 1-12. *Cloning the part*

Another way to place the part from the building palette is to drag and drop the part to the desired location on the build plate.

Moving a Part

After placing the part on the build plate, if you want to move the part to another location, then you need to first select the part; after selecting, the part will be highlighted with a blue outline, as shown in Figure 1-13. After that, start to drag the part. Once the part is in motion, the part will be highlighted with a green outline, as shown in Figure 1-14. Then you can move the part to the desired location on the build plate and drop the part.

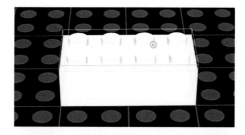

Figure 1-13. *Selected part shown with blue outline*

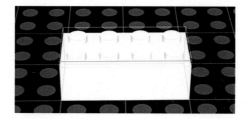

Figure 1-14. *Part in motion shown with the green outline*

You can also move the part using WASD keys.

Rotating a Part

For rotating a part, first you need to select the part. After selecting, the part will be highlighted with a blue outline, as shown in Figure 1-15. Then use the arrow keys to rotate in the desired direction, as shown on Figures 1-16 and 1-17.

Figure 1-15. *Selected part shown with blue outline*

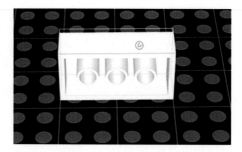

Figure 1-16. *Rotating a part using arrow keys*

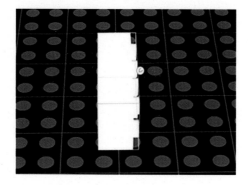

Figure 1-17. *Rotating a part using arrow keys*

Zoom In, Zoom Out, and Zoom to Fit

To zoom in and zoom out, you can scroll up and scroll down. You can also zoom in and zoom out through **View ➤ Zoom In**, **View ➤ Zoom Out**; you can fit the part or model in the screen through **View ➤ Zoom to Fit**, as shown in Figure 1-18.

Figure 1-18. *Zoom in/Zoom out*

Rotate Camera

To rotate the camera, hold down the right mouse button and move the mouse in the direction of rotation.

Pan Camera

To pan the camera, hold down the s**pace bar**, **right mouse button** and move the mouse in the direction of panning.

Changing the Orientation of View

To change the orientation of view, you need to click the viewport option, as shown in Figure 1-19. You can also change the orientation of view through **View ➤ Orientation**, as shown in Figure 1-20. You can switch the orientation to Free View, Front View, Back View, Left View, Right View, Bottom View, Top View, and Orthogonal View.

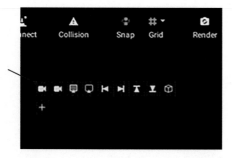

Figure 1-19. *Viewport controls*

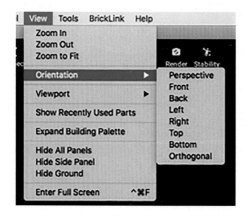

Figure 1-20. *Viewport controls through file option*

Add a Viewport

To add a viewport, you need to click the viewport option, as shown in Figure 1-21.
Choose the add viewport option to add a new viewport, as shown in Figure 1-22.

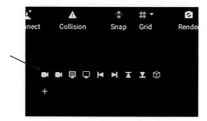

Figure 1-21. *Viewport controls*

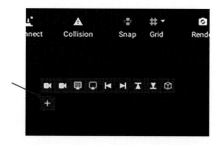

Figure 1-22. *Add a viewport*

You can also add a viewport through **View ➤ Viewport ➤ Add Viewport**, as shown in Figure 1-23. You can add a maximum of four viewports, as shown in Figure 1-24.

Figure 1-23. *Add a viewport through view*

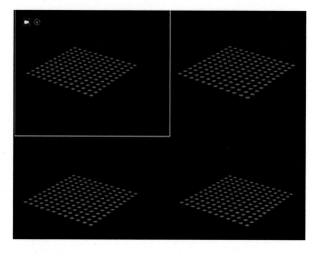

Figure 1-24. *Four viewports*

Delete a Viewport

After adding a viewport, if you want to delete the extra viewports, then you need to click **Delete Viewport Option**, as shown in Figure 1-25.

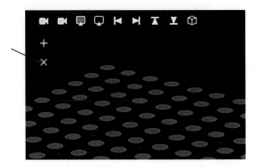

Figure 1-25. *Delete a viewport*

Viewport Rotation Lock

After setting the viewport to some particular orientation, if you want to lock that orientation, then you can click the viewport rotation lock option, as shown in Figure 1-26. After activating this lock, if you try to change the view, it will start displaying **The viewport rotation lock is on**.

Figure 1-26. *Viewport rotation lock*

Conclusion

In this chapter, you learned the basics of getting started with Studio 2.0. Now you can start a new project, move and rotate the parts, see the parts from different orientations, etc.

In the next chapter, you will learn about the different building tools, which will be very useful in designing models.

CHAPTER 2

Building Tools

In this chapter, you will explore all the building tools of Studio 2.0, as shown in
Figure 2-1. Which will be very useful and helpful in building the LEGO models.

Figure 2-1. *Building tools*

There are eight building tools: **Select, Hinge, Clone, Hide, Connect, Collision,
Snap, and Grid**. We will see each one of them in detail one by one.

Select Tool

When you click the arrow next to the select icon you will get six **select tool** options, that
is, **Default Select, By Color, By Type, By Type and Color, By Connected, and Invert
Selection**, as shown in Figure 2-2.

© Vishnu Agarwal 2023
V. Agarwal, *The Art of Virtual LEGO Design*, https://doi.org/10.1007/978-1-4842-8777-4_2

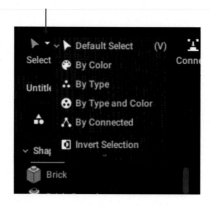

Figure 2-2. *Select tool*

- **Default Select**

The **default selection** tool is used to select any other tools or options in Studio 2.0. You also use the default tool to place, move, or rotate the parts.

- **By Color**

By Color select tool can be used to select all parts of the same color as the selected brick. It does not matter what the shape or size of the brick is, this tool will select all the parts of the same color. As shown in Figure 2-3, all red color bricks are selected using the By Color select tool, irrespective of shape and size. Selected bricks are shown with a blue color outline.

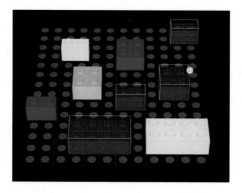

Figure 2-3. *Example of By Color select tool*

- **By Type**

By Type select tool can be used to select all parts of the same shape and size as the selected brick. It does not matter what the color of the brick is, this tool will select all the parts of the same shape and size. As shown in Figure 2-4, all 1*2 bricks are selected using the By Type select tool, irrespective of color. Selected bricks are shown with a blue color outline.

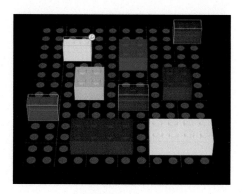

Figure 2-4. *Example of By Type select tool*

- **By Type and Color**

By Type and color select tool can be used to select all parts of the same shape and size and color as the selected brick. As shown in Figure 2-5, all 1*2 red bricks are selected using the By Type and Color select tool. Selected bricks are shown with a blue color outline.

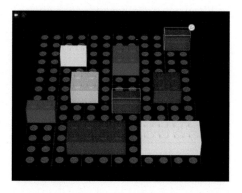

Figure 2-5. *Example of By Type and Color select tool*

- **By Connected**

By Connected select tool can be used to select all parts that are connected to the selected brick. It does not matter what the color, shape, or size of the bricks is. As shown in Figure 2-6, all the bricks which are connected to 2*4 yellow brick are selected by using the **By Connected** select tool. Selected bricks are shown with a blue color outline.

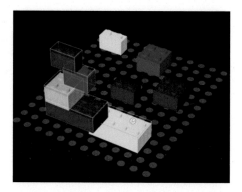

Figure 2-6. *Example of By Connected select tool*

- **Invert Selection**

Invert Selection tool selects the opposite of currently selected parts. Before you use the Invert Selection tool, select all the red bricks using the default select tool, as shown in Figure 2-7. To select the multiple bricks, press and hold the control/command button and select the bricks you want using the mouse left button. Then select the **Invert Selection** tool. The Invert selection tool will unselect previously selected parts and select rest of the parts, as shown in Figure 2-8. Selected bricks are shown with a blue color outline.

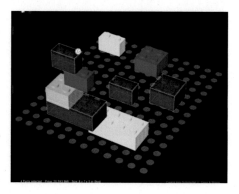

Figure 2-7. *Before using Invert Selection tool*

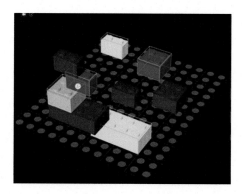

Figure 2-8. *After using Invert Selection tool*

Hinge Tool

To understand the hinge tool effectively, I will use a Minifigure. Drag and drop the following Minifigure parts on the building plate, as shown in Figure 2-9.

Figure 2-9. *Minifigure parts*

- Hair
- Head
- Torso
- Arms
- Hands
- Legs

Then assemble all the parts to make a Minifigure, as shown in Figure 2-10.

Figure 2-10. *Minifigure after assembling the parts*

Now select the hinge tool, as shown in Figure 2-11. Select the part of the Minifigure you would like to rotate. I will first select the arm of the Minifigure. When you will select the arm, you will get two axis of rotation (blue arrow) through which you can rotate the arm, as shown in Figure 2-12. When you will click on axis-1 (blue arrow) you will get one yellow cube and a blue arrow, as shown in Figure 2-13.

Figure 2-11. *Hinge tool*

Figure 2-12. *Axis of rotation for arm*

Figure 2-13. *Hinge of the selected parts, axis-1*

The yellow cube represents the hinge and the parts highlighted with blue color will rotate along with the hinge. The blue color arrow can be used to turn the part up and down.

There are two ways to turn the selected part. The first way is you can put the mouse pointer on the blue arrow; it will change to a red arrow and then click, hold, and drag the red arrow to rotate the Minifigure arm, as shown in Figure 2-14.

Figure 2-14. *Turing the part arm using arrow*

Another way to rotate the Minifigure arm is to put the mouse pointer on the blue arrow, and it will change to a red arrow and then click on that arrow. It will change to a circular angle with an angle input box option, as shown in Figure 2-15.

Figure 2-15. *Turning the arm by typing the angle value*

I have typed 90 degrees in the input box. After that, press enter. The Minifigure arm will turn at a 90-degree angle, as shown in Figure 2-16.

Figure 2-16. *After turning the arm by 90 degrees*

When you click on-axis-2 (blue arrow), as shown in Figure 2-17, you will get one yellow cube and a blue arrow, as shown in Figure 2-18.

Figure 2-17. *Axis of rotation for arm*

Figure 2-18. *Hinge of the selected parts, axis-2*

But in this case, a yellow cube which is the hinge of the selected part is at the joint of the arm and hand of Minifigure. So if you select the axis-2, along with the arm other body parts of the Minifigure will also be selected automatically, as shown in Figure 2-18, and whole body parts except the hand will rotate along the hinge (yellow cube), as shown in Figure 2-19. So be careful in selecting the right axis of rotation.

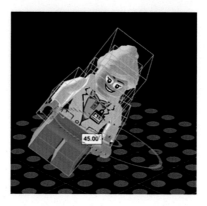

Figure 2-19. *After turning the parts*

Also, selecting multiple parts before using any tool can combine its effects.

Manual Mode

When you select any part on the building plate, you can see the **Minifigure hand icon** for the manual mode, as shown in Figure 2-20. When you hover over the icon, it will show you two available options: **Rotate (left)** and **Translate (right),** as shown in Figure 2-21.

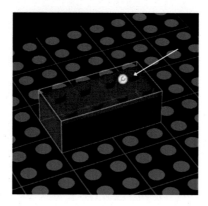

Figure 2-20. *Minifigure hand icon*

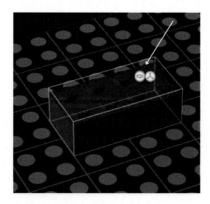

Figure 2-21. *Rotate and translate icons*

- **Rotate**

In the manual mode of the rotate option, you can do all the things that you can do using Hinge tool.

When you click on the rotate icon, you will get three blue arrows for the axis, as shown in Figure 2-22. Select the axis to rotate the selected part.

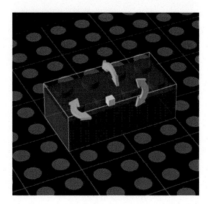

Figure 2-22. *Axis of rotation*

You can also rotate the part by typing the angle value in the input box, as shown in Figure 2-23.

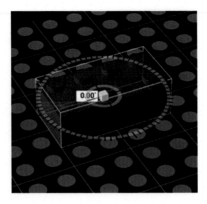

Figure 2-23. *Rotate the part using input box*

- **Translate**

When you click on the translate icon, you will get X, Y, and Z-axes to move the selected part, as shown in Figure 2-24. Select the axis to move and drag in the corresponding direction of the selected axis

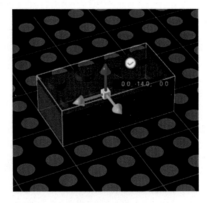

Figure 2-24. *Translate in the X, Y, and Z-axes*

Clone Tool

Clone tool can be used to make copies of selected part(s). For making a duplicate of a part(s), you need to select the part(s) and select the clone tool, or first, you can select the clone tool and then select the part(s) you want to clone, as shown in Figure 2-25.

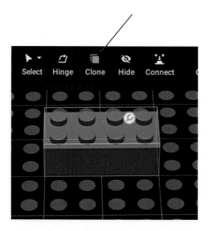

Figure 2-25. *Select the part for clone*

After that, you will get a duplicate of the selected part(s). You can move the part(s) to the desired location on the build plate and drop the part(s), as shown in Figure 2-26.

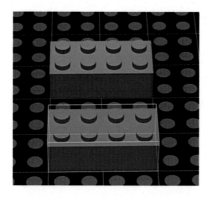

Figure 2-26. *After cloning the part*

After dropping the part(s) on the build plate, the part(s) will stick to the mouse pointer and start giving you a copy of the part. To get rid of this, you can right-click or press the ESC button.

Hide Tool

Hide tool can be used to hide the selected part(s). For hiding the part(s), you need to select the part(s) and select the hide tool, or first you can select the hide tool and then select the part(s) you want to hide, as shown in Figure 2-27.

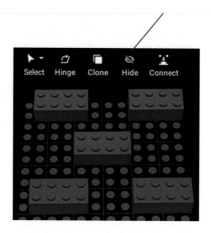

Figure 2-27. *Select the part(s) for hiding*

After using the hide tool, all the selected part(s) will disappear from the screen. But actually, the parts are not deleted but only hidden. On the right top corner of the port view window, you can get the count of hidden parts. You can click on **show all** to get all the hidden parts back, as shown in Figure 2-28.

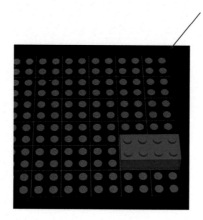

Figure 2-28. *After hiding the part*

To get rid of Hide Tool, press the ESC button.

Connect Tool

For demonstrating how to use the connect tool, I have used two 2*2 LEGO bricks. Now select the connect tool and select the left 2*2 LEGO brick. After selecting the brick, it will show you all the connection points like studs, anti studs, and tube connections, as shown in Figure 2-29.

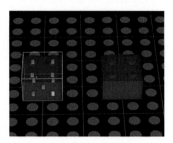

Figure 2-29. *Select the follower's connection point*

The first part which you will select behaves like a follower and the second part will behave like a target.

After selecting a connection point on the left brick (follower), you have to move the mouse pointer to the brick where you want to connect the first brick. In this case, we will move to the second 2*2 brick (target). As soon as you start moving the mouse pointer from left brick (follower) to right brick (target) one green color wire will also come along with the mouse pointer and when you reach the right brick you will see all the connection points possible to connect the left brick, as shown in Figure 2-30. The green wire will help you to understand where the follower connection point will connect to the target connection point.

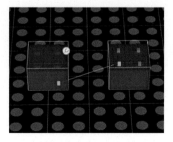

Figure 2-30. *Select the target's connection point*

After selecting the connection point on the second brick (target), the first brick (follower) will automatically snap to the target brick at the selected connection point, as shown in Figure 2-31.

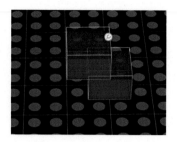

Figure 2-31. *After using the connect tool*

To get rid of Connect Tool, press the ESC button.

Collision

The Collision tool is used to check if the parts are colliding with each other or not.

To understand the collision tool, let's take two 2*4 bricks on the building plate and turn on the **collision detection** option, as shown in Figure 2-32. Now select the left 2*4 brick and use **key-D** to move the brick toward another 2*4 brick. As soon as both the 2*4 bricks collide with each other they become semi-transparent, as shown in Figure 2-33.

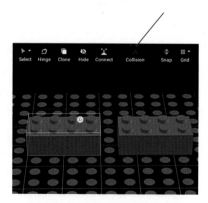

Figure 2-32. *Two 2*4 bricks on the building plate*

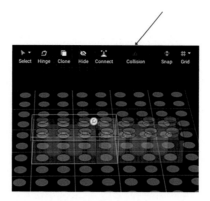

Figure 2-33. *Two 2*4 bricks colliding with each other*

The collision detection option is very important when you are working on big models. It will help you to minimize mistakes.

Snap

To understand the Snap tool, let's take two 2*4 bricks on the building plate and turn on the **Snap** option, as shown in Figure 2-34.

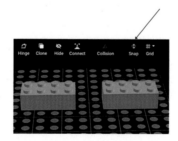

Figure 2-34. *Two 2*4 bricks on the building plate*

Now select the left 2*4 brick and drag it to connect on the second 2*4 brick. The first brick will automatically snap on the second brick, as shown in Figure 2-35.

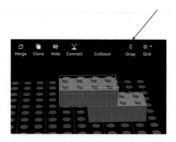

Figure 2-35. *Connect two bricks (Snap ON)*

Now, turn off the Snap option and try to connect the left 2*4 brick to right 2*4 brick. If you try to do that the first brick will not snap automatically. You need to put a lot of effort to align the brick and only then both bricks will snap. If bricks are not placed properly they collide with each other, as shown in Figure 2-36.

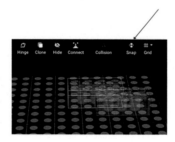

Figure 2-36. *Connect two bricks (Snap OFF)*

Grid

The grid option is used to move the parts in X, Y, and Z directions with different measurements using W, S, A, D keys or the Transition option.

There are four options in the grid: Coarse, Medium, Medium Plate, and Fine.

To understand the grid options, I have used one 2*2 brick and three 2*2 plates, as shown in Figure 2-37.

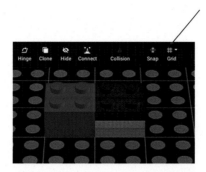

Figure 2-37. *Explanation of Grid options using bricks and plates*

- **Coarse Grid**

When you move the blue 2*2 brick in the **coarse grid** mode using the transition option, the brick will move one entire stud in all directions (X, Y, and Z axes), as shown in Figure 2-38.

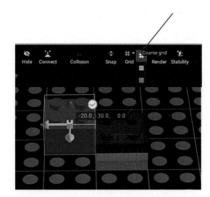

Figure 2-38. *Top view of bricks in coarse grid*

But if you move the brick using W, S, A, D keys, the brick should be in the top view to move one entire stud in X and Y axes, and side view if you want to move the brick one entire stud on Z-axis, as shown in Figure 2-39.

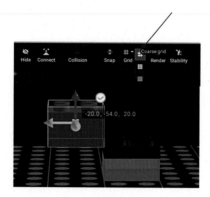

Figure 2-39. *Side view of bricks in coarse grid*

- **Medium Grid**

When you move the blue 2*2 brick in the **medium grid** mode using the transition option, the brick will move one-half stud in all directions (X, Y, and Z axes), as shown in Figure 2-40.

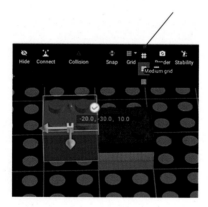

Figure 2-40. *Top view of bricks in medium grid*

But if you move the brick using W, S, A, D keys, the brick should be in the top view to move one-half stud in X and Y axes, and side view if you want to move the brick one-half stud on Z-axis, as shown in Figure 2-41.

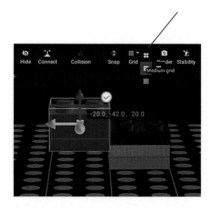

Figure 2-41. *Side view of bricks in medium grid*

- **Medium Plate Grid**

When you move the blue 2*2 brick in the **medium plate grid** mode using the transition option, the brick will still move one-half stud on X and Y axes but moves the height of one plate on Z-axis, as shown in Figure 2-42.

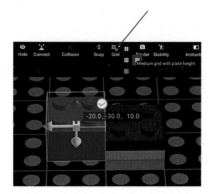

Figure 2-42. *Top view of bricks in medium plate grid*

If you move the brick using W, S, A, D keys, then the brick should be in the top view to move one-half stud in X and Y axes and side view if you want to move the brick the height of one plate on Z-axis, as shown in Figure 2-43.

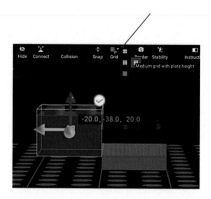

Figure 2-43. *Side view of bricks in medium plate grid*

- **Fine Grid**

When you move the blue 2*2 brick in the **fine grid** mode using the transition option, the brick will move in a very small amount, much smaller than 1/4 stud in all directions (X, Y, and Z axes), as shown in Figure 2-44.

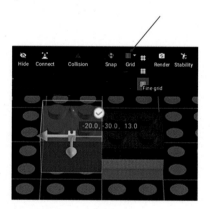

Figure 2-44. *Top view of bricks in fine grid*

But if you move the brick using W, S, A, D keys, then the brick should be in the top view to move on X and Y axes and side view if you want to move the brick on Z-axis, as shown in Figure 2-45.

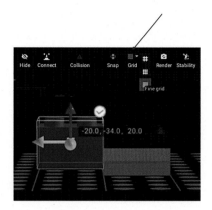

Figure 2-45. *Side view of bricks in fine grid*

Conclusion

In this chapter, you learned all the building tools. As you will use all these building tools from basic to advanced models, you should have very good command over these building tools. So make sure you understand each and every concept in this chapter before you move to the next chapter.

In the next chapter, you will explore all the Bricks Palette, which will help you to find and manage LEGO bricks easily.

CHAPTER 3

Building Palette

In this chapter, you will learn to **filter, categorize**, **and search** the parts. It is the most important skill to increase your speed of building LEGO models. If you are able to search parts quickly, then you will be able to finish the model fast.

The building palette will provide you access to almost the entire BrickLink catalog of LEGO parts. The building palette is present on the left-hand side (vertical position) of the Studio 2.0 software, as shown in Figure 3-1. The position of the building palette can also be changed to the bottom (horizontal) of Studio 2.0, which we will learn in Chapter 8.

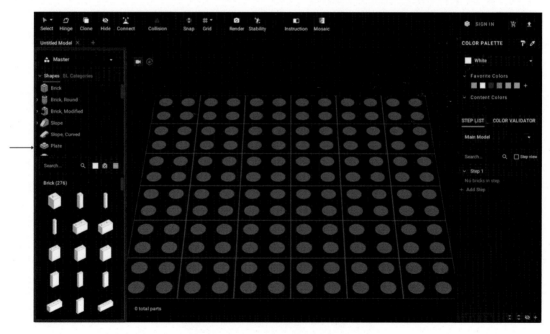

Figure 3-1. *Building Palette*

© Vishnu Agarwal 2023
V. Agarwal, *The Art of Virtual LEGO Design*, https://doi.org/10.1007/978-1-4842-8777-4_3

Master

The first way to filter the parts is using a pre-built parts palette. The first pre-built parts palette is Master Palette. By default, the Master palette is selected in the building palette, as shown in Figure 3-2.

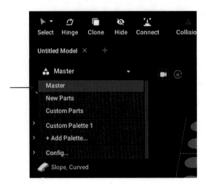

Figure 3-2. *Selecting Master Palette*

After selecting the Master Palette, the building palette will look like as is shown in Figure 3-3. The master palette will provide you access to almost the entire BrickLink catalog of LEGO parts.

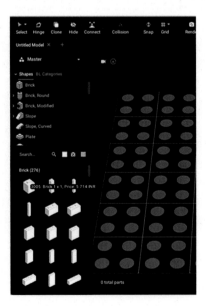

Figure 3-3. *After Selecting the Master Palette*

You can also check the part's number, name, and price by moving the mouse pointer on each part, as shown in Figure 3-3.

New Parts

Another way to filter the parts is using the second pre-built parts palette, **New Parts**, as shown in Figure 3-4.

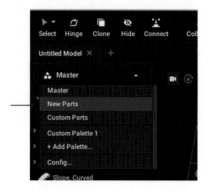

Figure 3-4. *Selecting New Parts palette*

In the New Parts palette, you will get all the parts which have recently been added to the Studio.

After selecting the New Parts palette, the building palette will look like as shown in Figure 3-5.

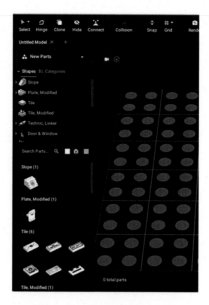

Figure 3-5. *After selecting the New Parts palette*

You can also check the part's number, name, and price by moving the mouse pointer on each part.

Custom Parts

Another way to filter the parts is using the third pre-built parts palette, **Custom parts**, as shown in Figure 3-6.

Figure 3-6. *Selecting Custom Parts palette*

In the Custom Parts palette, you will get all the parts which are designed in the **PartDesigner** software. PartDesigner is another software by BrickLink which can be used to design custom parts.

After selecting the Custom Parts palette the building palette will look like as is shown in Figure 3-5. I have created a few custom parts using PartDesigner, as shown in Figure 3-7.

Figure 3-7. *After selecting the Custom Parts palette*

Hidden Parts

Using the hide option, you can hide any part from the palette. To hide any part, you need to right-click on that part, after that you will get an option to hide the part, as shown in Figure 3-8.

41

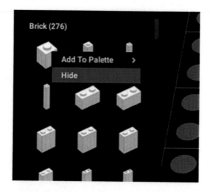

Figure 3-8. *Option for hiding the part*

After selecting the hide option, one window pops up which says "The selected part has been hidden successfully." You can browse all hidden parts in the "Hidden Parts" palette and restore, as shown in Figure 3-9.

Figure 3-9. *After selecting the hide option*

To browse all the hidden parts, you need to click the hidden parts palette, as shown in Figure 3-10. In this palette, you will get all the parts that you hid.

Figure 3-10. *Browse hidden parts*

After clicking the hidden parts palette, you can see there is one 1*1 brick available, as shown in Figure 3-10, which we hid using the hide option, as shown in Figure 3-8.

We can also restore the part by right-clicking the part and selecting the restore option, as shown in Figure 3-11.

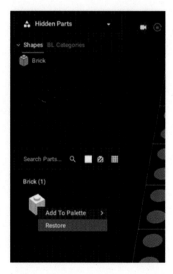

Figure 3-11. *Restore hidden parts*

Custom Palette

To add a custom palette, you need to click +Add Palette, as shown in Figure 3-12.

Figure 3-12. *Adding a custom palette*

After that, one window will pop up. It will ask you to give a name for your custom palette. The default name will be "Custom Palette 1." You can select the type for your custom palette and click Okay to create the custom palette, as shown in Figure 3-13.

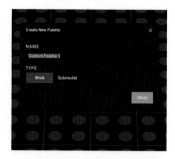

Figure 3-13. *Name the custom palette*

After creating the empty custom palette it will look like as shown in Figure 3-14.

Figure 3-14. *Empty custom palette*

To add a part to the custom palette, you need to right-click any part in the Master Palette or any other palette, as shown in Figure 3-15. You can select the pre-made palette

and add that part or click on **New Palette** to create a new custom palette and the part
to that.

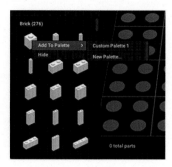

Figure 3-15. *Adding parts to custom palette*

To open the custom palette, you need to click the palette name which you created, as
shown in Figure 3-16.

Figure 3-16. *Opening the custom palette*

After opening that palette, you will see all the parts that you added to this palette.
You can also delete the part by right-clicking the part and selecting Delete, as shown in
Figure 3-17.

Figure 3-17. *Deleting parts from custom palette*

Import an Official LEGO Set

To import an official LEGO set to the Studio, you need to select the last option "Configure" in the parts palette section, as shown in Figure 3-18.

Figure 3-18. *Select Configure option*

After that, a new window will appear where you need to click "Choose a way to add new palette" and then select the option "Import an official LEGO set," as shown in Figure 3-19.

Figure 3-19. *Selecting Import an official LEGO set option*

After that, another window will appear where you need to type the official LEGO set number, as shown in Figure 3-20. If you do not know the set number, then you can click "view catalog" to see the set number. After typing the correct set number, you can see the set preview.

Figure 3-20. *Typing LEGO set number*

After that, you need to select the import type. If you want the set to import into the scene (on the building plate) then select "in scene" and if you want the set to import into a palette then select "as palette."

In the end, you will also get the option for "Include minifig parts" and "Extra parts." If you want to add these parts to your import then select it, otherwise unselect it.

Once you are done selecting your preferred options, click on "Import."

After clicking on "Import," as shown in Figure 3-20, you will get another window that shows parts which are failed to import. You can check the list and then click Okay, as shown in Figure 3-21. For the parts which failed to import, you can search for those parts in the Master palette.

Figure 3-21. *Parts which are failed to import*

Once the set has been imported, it will appear as a palette in the parts palette section. I have imported the LEGO Mindstorms EV3 robotics set (45544), which you can see in the parts palette, as shown in Figure 3-22.

Figure 3-22. *After importing an official LEGO set*

Part Categories

There are two ways you can categorize the parts. The first way is by the shape and size of the parts. It categorizes the parts based on their appearance. For example, **Brick: Brick, Round; Brick, Modified; Slope: Slope, Curved, etc.,** as shown in Figure 3-23.

Figure 3-23. *Categorizes the parts using shapes*

Another way to categorize the parts is using Bricklink categories. Bricklink uses the same categories on Bricklink.com. For example, **Aircraft; Animals; Antenna; Arm; Ball; Bar, etc.**, as shown in Figure 3-24.

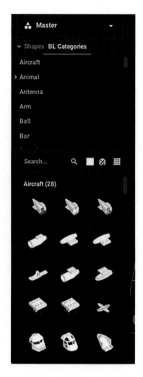

Figure 3-24. *BrickLink Categories of the parts*

FAVORITE PARTS

If you hover your mouse pointer over any parts folder, then you will see a star mark at the side of the folder name, as shown in Figure 3-25.

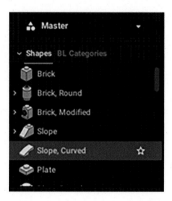

Figure 3-25. *Before selecting the favourite parts folder*

If you want to add any parts folder to your favorite list, then click on this star and that folder will be added at the start of the parts folder and it will be highlighted with the star mark, as shown in Figure 3-26.

Figure 3-26. *After selecting the favourite parts folder*

Searching Parts Using Keywords

Last and the most important way to filter the parts is by using the search bar, as shown in Figure 3-27. You can search by typing the part number or part name. If you do not know the exact name or number of parts, then you can type the characteristics of the part. For example, if you have to search **Slope 45 2x2 brick (3039)** and you do not know the part number and name then you can type something similar names like **slope 2.** Then Studio will show you all the parts which are partially similar to the description, as shown in Figure 3-28. After that, you can scroll the parts palette and select the correct part.

Figure 3-27. *Search bar*

Figure 3-28. *Searching slope bricks*

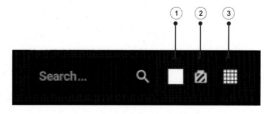

Figure 3-29. *Parts palette display options*

To the right side of the search bar, you will get three options to customize the parts palette as shown in Figure 3-29.

1. Palette color

2. Decorated bricks on/off

3. Thumbnail size

1. Palette Colors

When you click on the palette colors option, you will get a palette to select the color for the parts, as shown in Figure 3-30. After selecting the color, all the parts available in the parts palette will be available in that color, as shown in Figure 3-31.

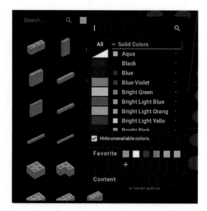

Figure 3-30. *Palette color options*

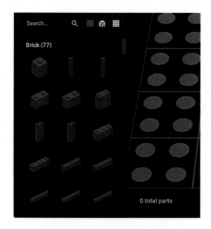

Figure 3-31. *After selecting the palette color*

2. Decorated Bricks On/Off

Using the decorated bricks option, you can turn on/off the decorated parts in the parts palette. If you turn it ON, then it will show you all the decorated parts available in the parts palette. For example, as shown in Figure 3-32, all the 1*1 LEGO brick decorated parts are available. If you turn it OFF, then it will show you only non-decorated parts.

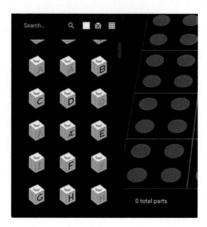

Figure 3-32. *Decorated bricks*

3. Thumbnail Size

The Thumbnail size option will allow you to change the size of the parts available in the parts palette. You can change the size of the parts to small, medium, and large, as shown in Figures 3-33, 3-34, and 3-35.

Figure 3-33. *Parts size: small*

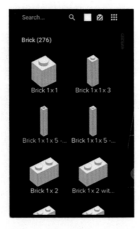

Figure 3-34. *Parts size: medium*

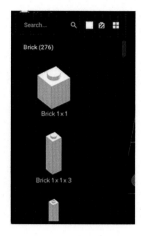

Figure 3-35. *Parts size: large*

Conclusion

In this chapter, you learned all the pre-build parts palettes, that is, Master, New parts, and custom parts. You also learned how to create a custom palette and import official LEGO sets. After that, you saw how to categorize the parts based on shape and Bricklink category. And at last, you learned how to search the parts using keywords and a few more important features.

In the next chapter, you will explore the color palette option. As color plays an important role in building models, we will see all the color options available in the Studio.

CHAPTER 4

Color Palette

In this chapter, you will explore the "Color Palette" option. The color palette is situated at the top right corner of the software, as shown in Figure 4-1. As color plays an important role in building models, we will see all the color options available in the Studio.

Figure 4-1. *Color palette*

You will learn about a few features of the color palette, that is, painting with the selected color, grabbing color from parts, favorite colors, content colors, different types of colors, and hiding unavailable colors.

Painting with Selected Color

You can use the "Paint with selected color" option to change the color of bricks. First, you need to select the desired color from the color options, as shown in Figure 4-2. After that, select the "Paint with selected color" option, as shown in Figure 4-3.

© Vishnu Agarwal 2023
V. Agarwal, *The Art of Virtual LEGO Design*, https://doi.org/10.1007/978-1-4842-8777-4_4

Figure 4-2. *Select the color*

Figure 4-3. *Painting with selected color option*

After that, the mouse pointer will convert into a painting roller and then you can click the parts of which you want to change the color, as shown in Figure 4-4. I have used the bright light orange color.

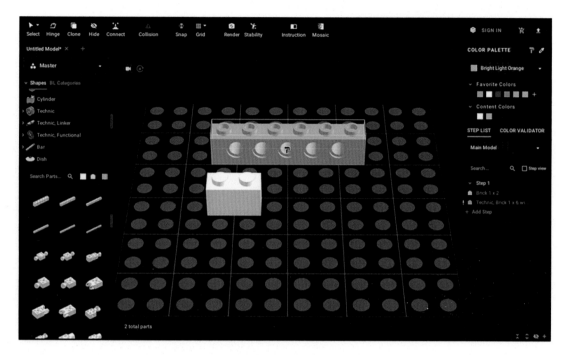

Figure 4-4. *Painting with selected color option*

We can also change the color of the parts by first selecting the parts and then selecting the desired color. As shown in Figure 4-5, I have first selected the 1*2 white brick. Then I have selected the blue color option in the color palette to change the 1*2 brick color from white to blue, as shown in Figure 4-6.

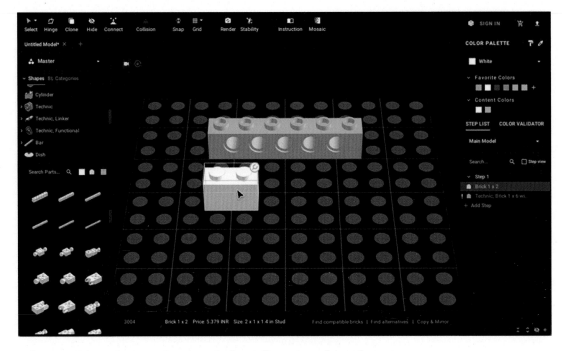

Figure 4-5. *Selecting the part before changing the color*

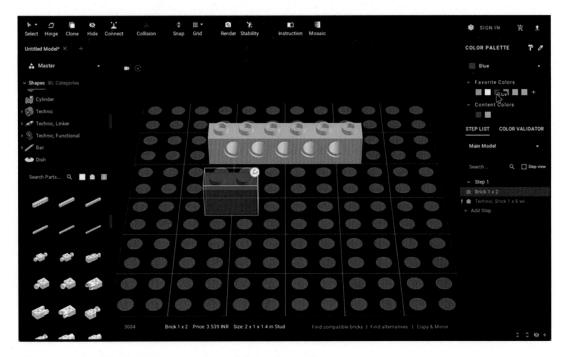

Figure 4-6. *Changing the color of the selected part*

Grab Color from Part

To grab the color from a part, first you need to select the "Grab color from part" option, as shown in Figure 4-7. Then move the mouse pointer to the part whose color you want to grab and click that part. As shown in Figure 4-8, I have clicked fabuland pastel green 2*2 brick, and then the selected color will also change from bright light orange to the fabuland pastel green.

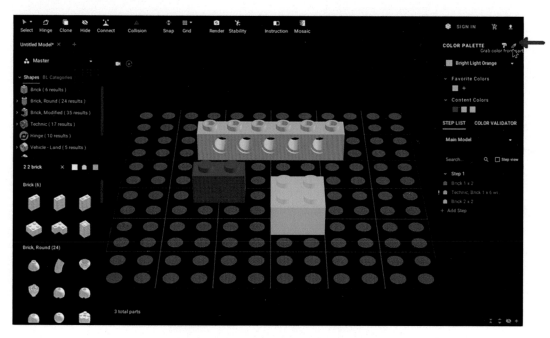

Figure 4-7. *Selecting the grab color from part option*

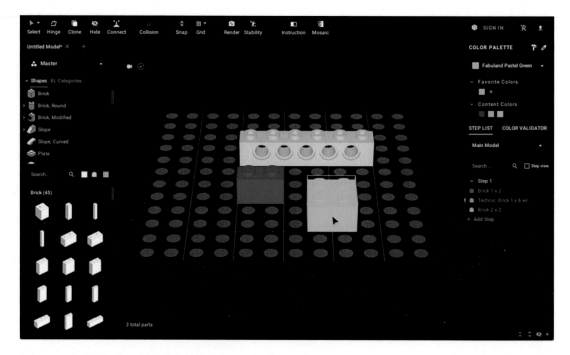

Figure 4-8. *Selecting the part to grab the color*

Now you can use the "Paint with selected color" option to change the color of other parts to fabuland pastel green, as shown in Figures 4-9 and 4-10.

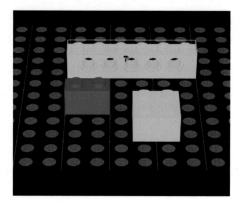

Figure 4-9. *Changing the part color*

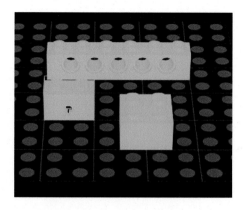

Figure 4-10. *Changing the part color*

Colors List

You can click on the colors list option to open all the colors available in the bricklink, as shown in Figure 4-11. Clicking it will open the list of colors, as shown in Figure 4-12.

Figure 4-11. *Colors list option*

Figure 4-12. *List of colors*

You will get fifteen different colors folders, that is, Solid colors, Transparent colors, Chrome colors, Pearl colors, Metallic colors, Milky Colors, Glitter colors, Speckle colors, Rubber colors, Satin colors, Glowing neon (Render only), Luminous soft (Render only), Luminous (Render only), Translucent (Render only) and Glow in dark (Render only).

- **Solid Colors**

Under solid colors palette, you will get around 88 different colors, as shown in Figure 4-13.

Figure 4-13. *Solid colors*

The total no. of available colors might change once you update the software.

- **Transparent Colors**

Under transparent colors palette, you will get around 22 different colors, as shown in Figure 4-14.

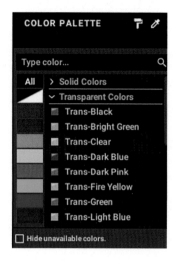

Figure 4-14. *Transparent colors*

The total no. of available colors might change once you update the software.

- **Chrome Colors**

Under the chrome colors palette, you will get around seven different colors, as shown in Figure 4-15.

Figure 4-15. *Chrome colors*

The total no. of available colors might change once you update the software.

- **Pearl Colors**

Under the pearl colors palette, you will get around 13 different colors, as shown in Figure 4-16.

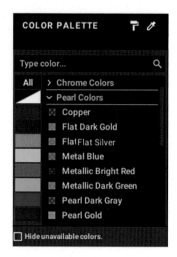

Figure 4-16. *Pearl colors*

The total no. of available colors might change once you update the software.

- **Metallic Colors**

Under the metallic colors palette, you will get around five different colors, as shown in Figure 4-17.

Figure 4-17. *Metallic colors*

The total no. of available colors might change once you update the software.

- **Milky Colors**

Under the milky colors palette, you will get around four different colors, as shown in Figure 4-18.

Figure 4-18. *Milky colors*

The total no. of available colors might change once you update the software.

- **Glitter Colors**

Under the metallic colors palette, you will get around seven different colors, as shown in Figure 4-19.

Figure 4-19. *Glitter colors*

The total no. of available colors might change once you update the software.

- **Speckle Colors**

Under the speckle colors palette, you will get around four different colors, as shown in Figure 4-20.

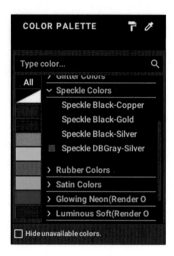

Figure 4-20. *Speckle colors*

The total no. of available colors might change once you update the software.

- **Rubber Colors**

Under the rubber colors palette, you will get around 32 different colors, as shown in Figure 4-21.

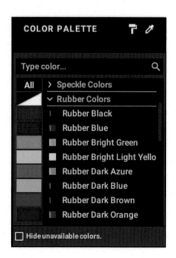

Figure 4-21. *Rubber colors*

The total no. of available colors might change once you update the software.

- **Satin Colors**

Under the satin colors palette, you will get around three different colors, as shown in Figure 4-22.

Figure 4-22. *Satin colors*

The total no. of available colors might change once you update the software.

- **Glowing Neon**

Under the glowing neon colors palette, you will get around eight different colors, as shown in Figure 4-23.

Figure 4-23. *Glowing Neon colors*

These colors are only for rendering. There are no real LEGO parts available in these colors.

The total no. of available colors might change once you update the software.

- **Luminous Soft**

Under the luminous soft colors palette, you will get around six different colors, as shown in Figure 4-24.

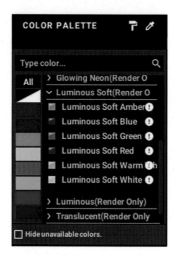

Figure 4-24. *Luminous soft colors*

These colors are only for rendering. There are no real LEGO parts available in these colors.

The total no. of available colors might change once you update the software.

WHAT DOES IT MEAN TO RENDER AN IMAGE?

Rendering is the process involved in the generation of a two-dimensional or three-dimensional image from a model by means of application programs

You will learn about how to render an image of the LEGO model in Chapter 6.

- **Luminous**

Under the luminous colors palette, you will get around ten colors, as shown in Figure 4-25.

Figure 4-25. *Luminous colors*

These colors are only for rendering. There are no real LEGO parts available in these colors.

The total no. of available colors might change once you update the software.

- **Translucent**

Under the translucent colors palette, you will get around eight different colors, as shown in Figure 4-26.

Figure 4-26. *Translucent colors*

These colors are only for rendering. There are no real LEGO parts available in these colors.

The total no. of available colors might change once you update the software.

- **Glow in Dark**

Under the glow-in-dark colors palette, you will get around 32 colors, as shown in Figure 4-27.

Figure 4-27. *Glow in Dark colors*

These colors are only for rendering. There are no real LEGO parts available in these colors.

The total no. of available colors might change once you update the software.

Selecting Colors by Shade

You can also select the color by shade type. For example, if you want to select all the colors which are of a yellow shade then you need to click the yellow color on the left side of the color palette and it will give you all the yellow shade colors across all the color folders, as shown in Figure 4-28.

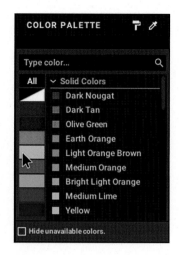

Figure 4-28. *Yellow color shades*

Hide Unavailable Colors

Hide unavailable color is an amazing feature in Studio 2.0 software. You can hide all the unavailable colors for a part.

I have dragged and dropped a 1*1 brick on the building plate and then selected the "Hide unavailable colors" option which is available at the bottom of the colors list palette; it will show you only the colors which are available for that part, as shown in Figure 4-29.

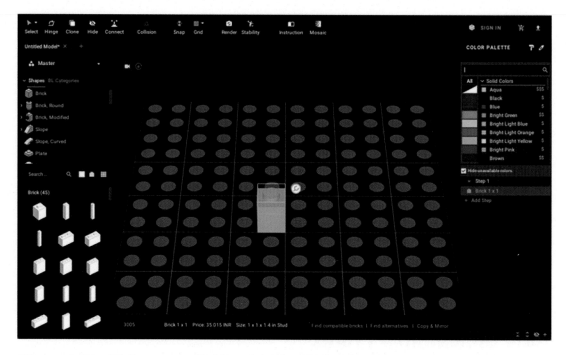

Figure 4-29. *Hiding unavailable colors for 1*1 brick*

Next to each color, the **$** symbol represents how expensive is that part. If you hover the mouse pointer on the color, it will also show the exact price of the part in that color.

For some parts, it will show you "ender only" colors also. But if you select that color you need to fix that in the "Color Validator" options shown in Figure 4-30.

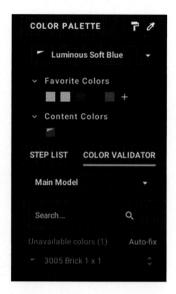

Figure 4-30. *Color Validator*

You will learn about Color Validator in Chapter 6.

Favorite Colors

You can add the selected color as a favorite color by pressing the "+" symbol under Favorite colors section, as shown in Figure 4-31.

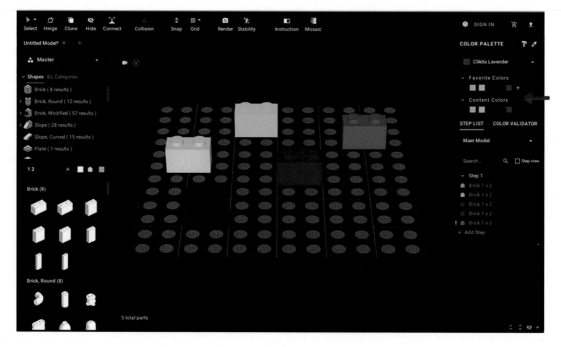

Figure 4-31. *Adding the selected color as a favorite color*

Content Colors

The Content Colors section under Color Palette will give you all the different part colors list available on the build plate for a particular model. Randomly, I have dragged and dropped 22 different color parts on the building plate and the Content Color is showing all the different colors, as shown in Figure 4-32.

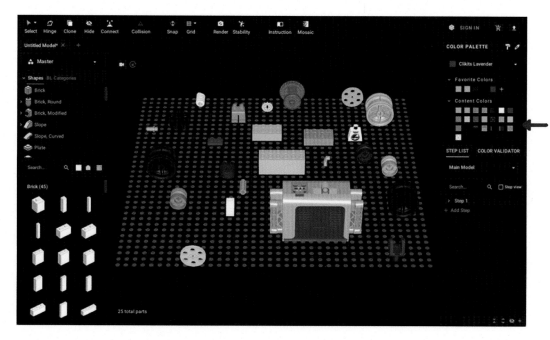

Figure 4-32. *Content Colors*

Conclusion

In this chapter, you learned about painting with the selected color, grab colors from parts, colors that are available only for rendering, hiding unavailable colors, and many other features available in the color palette.

In the next chapter, you will learn different design tools, which will make your work easier.

CHAPTER 5

Design Tools

In this chapter, I will explain some important design tools which will be helpful in building the model. For example, Find Compatible Bricks, find Alternatives, Copy and Mirror, Create into Submodel, Part no., Type, Price, and Size, as shown in Figure 5-1.

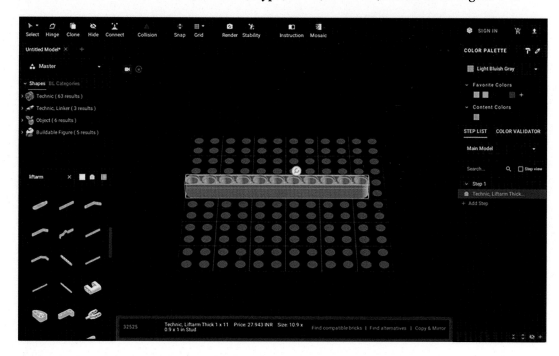

Figure 5-1. *Important features helpful for building models*

V. Agarwal, *The Art of Virtual LEGO Design*, https://doi.org/10.1007/978-1-4842-8777-4_5

Find Compatible Bricks

This option only implies some specific couple of parts that are supposed to work with each other. For instance, a wheel and appropriate tire, window frame and the appropriate glass for the door, hinge plate and the other side of the hinge plate, and many other combinations.

To find the compatible brick for the tire you need to first select the tire then click the "Find compatible bricks" option, and you can see the compatible parts for the tire in the bricks palette, as shown in Figure 5-2.

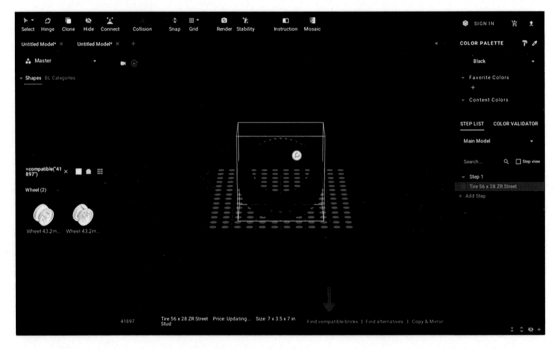

Figure 5-2. *Compatible bricks for tire*

It works in the same way for the other parts also. A few more examples are shown in Figures 5-3, 5-4, 5-5, 5-6, 5-7, and 5-8.

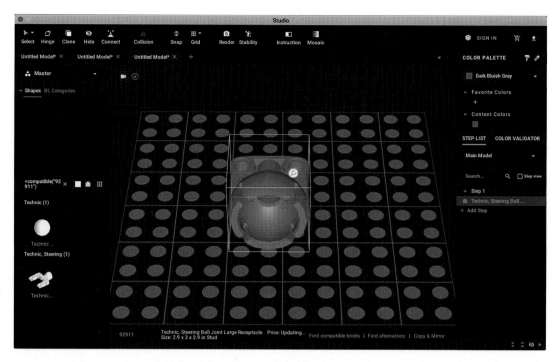

Figure 5-3. *Compatible bricks Steering Ball*

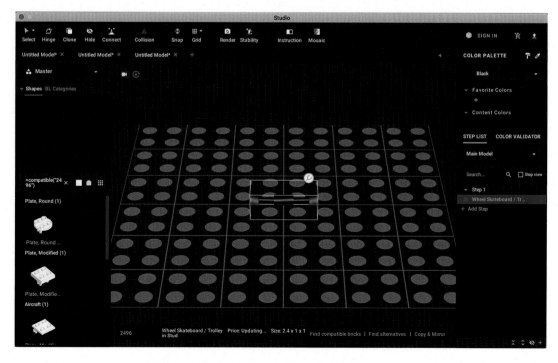

Figure 5-4. *Compatible bricks for Wheel Skateboard*

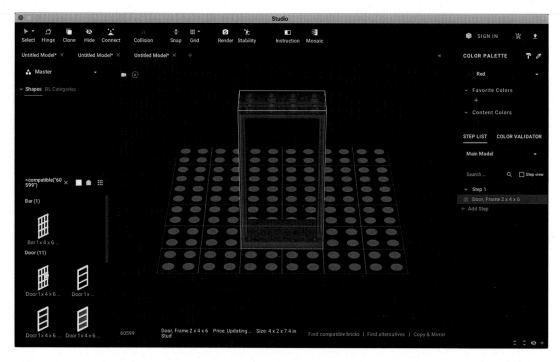

Figure 5-5. *Compatible bricks for Door*

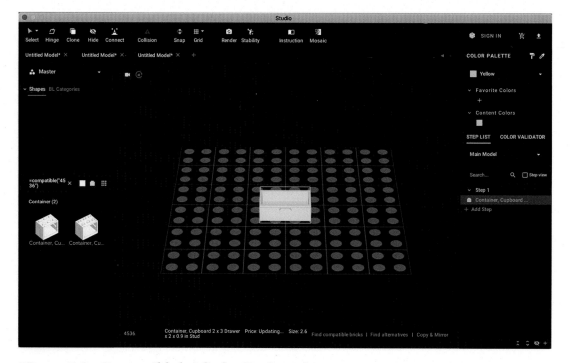

Figure 5-6. *Compatible bricks for Cupboard*

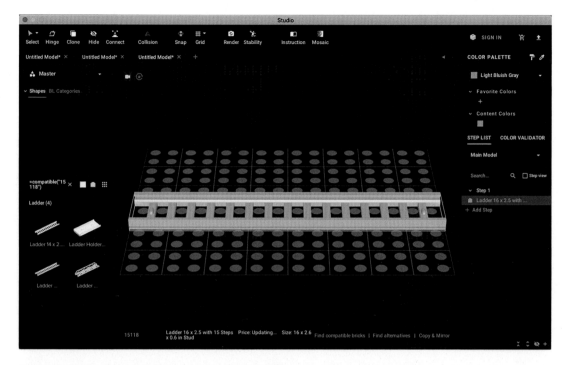

Figure 5-7. *Compatible bricks for Ladder*

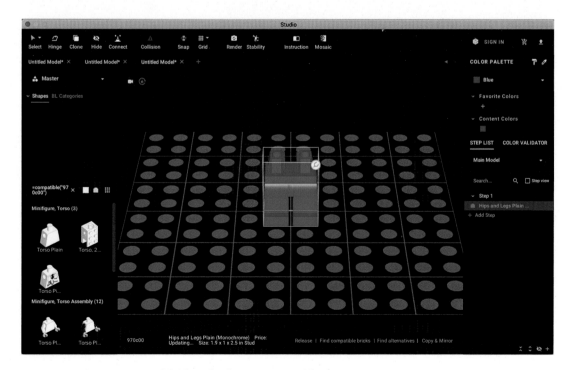

Figure 5-8. *Compatible bricks for Hips and legs*

Sometimes you will not see any compatible bricks for a part. It means that part is compatible with heaps of bricks and the Studio doesn't bother to show all the compatible bricks. For example, 2*4 brick is compatible with many other bricks so if you look for compatible bricks then it will not show anything in the bricks palette, as shown in Figure 5-9.

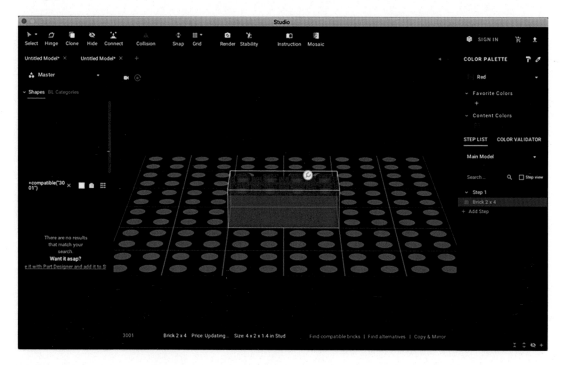

Figure 5-9. *Compatible bricks for 2*4 brick*

Find Alternatives

This options is used to search for any replacement of the part which might be a better fit for a model. If there are no alternative parts available, then it will show the same part in the bricks palette.

For example, I have selected the technic, brick modified 2*2 with 2 ball joints. After that, I clicked the "Find Alternatives" option. The Studio then showed all the alternate parts available in the bricks palette, as shown in Figure 5-10.

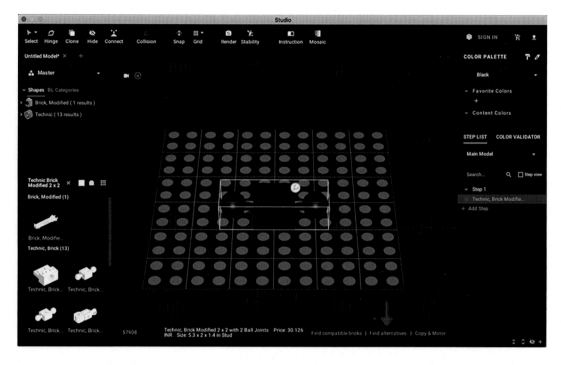

Figure 5-10. *Alternative bricks for technic, brick modified 2*2 with 2 ball joints*

Submodels

To create any group of parts into a submodel, first you need to select the parts you want to convert into a submodel and then click the option "Create into Submodel," which is present at the bottom of the software.

For example, I used three 2*4 bricks to make a random model and then I selected all three bricks and clicked "Create into Submodel," as shown in Figure 5-11.

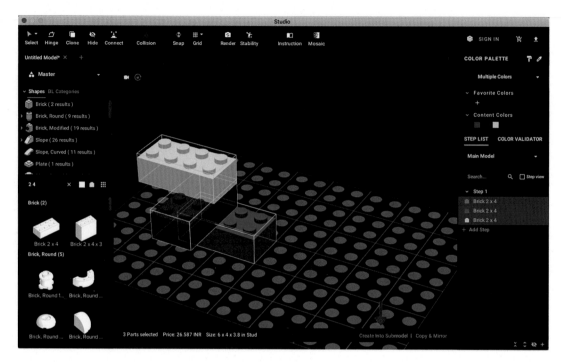

Figure 5-11. *Random model using 2*4 bricks*

After selecting the "Create into Submodel" option, a new window will open. You can type the desired name for your submodel, as shown in Figure 5-12.

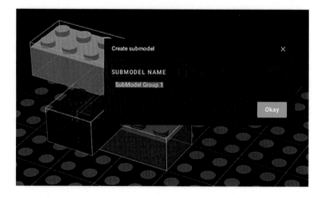

Figure 5-12. *Submodel name*

After giving the name to your submodel, the selected parts will convert into a submodel, as shown in Figure 5-13.

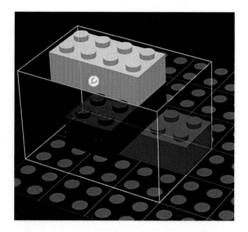

Figure 5-13. *Final Submodel*

Important

- The "Create into Submodel" option will be visible only when you select two or more parts.

- You cannot convert a single part into a submodel.

Edit, Release, and Unlink from Submodel

Edit, release, and unlink from submodel options will appear at the bottom of the screen after you create a submodel. Let's understand these options one by one, as seen in Figure 5-14.

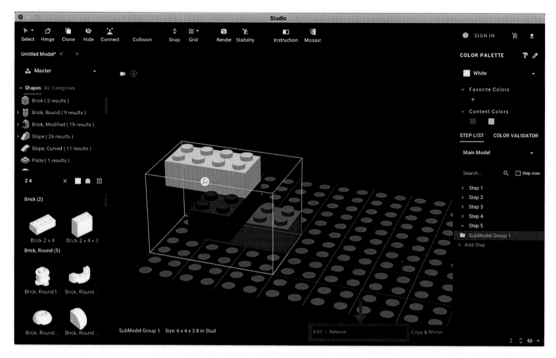

Figure 5-14. *Edit, release, and unlink from submodel options*

- **Edit**

After creating the submodel if you want to do any changes, that is, add, delete, or modify the parts in the submodel, then you can use the edit option.

In the previous model, as shown in Figure 5-14, if we want to add a white 2*4 brick, then first we need to click the "Edit" option, as shown in Figure 5-14. After that, you can add the 2*4 brick to the submodel as required, as shown in Figure 5-15.

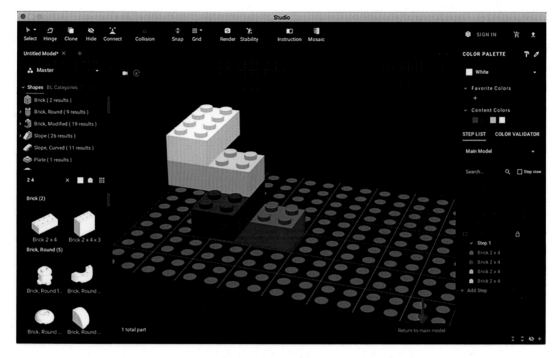

Figure 5-15. *Adding 2*4 white brick and return to main model option*

Once you are done with the required changes, click the "Return to main model" option available at the bottom of the screen, as shown in Figure 5-15.

- **Release**

The release option is used to convert the submodel back to the individual parts, as shown in Figure 5-16. The release option will be available at the bottom of the screen, as shown in Figure 5-14, and it appears only once you select any submodel.

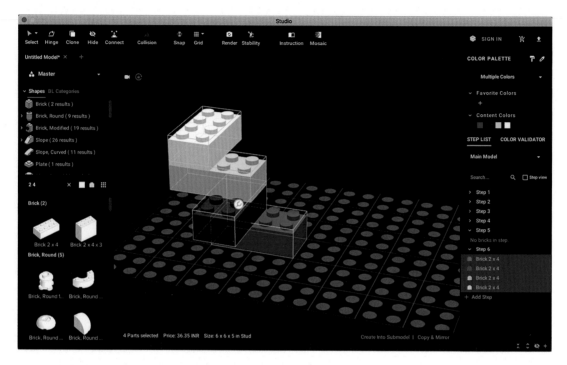

Figure 5-16. *After releasing the submodel*

- **Unlink from submodel**

If you make a copy of any existing submodel and make any changes in any of the submodels using the edit option without unlinking, then the changes will be applied to all the submodel copies.

If you unlink the copied submodels before editing, then it will behave as an independent submodel.

To understand what happens if you don't unlink from the submodel, use the submodel created in Figure 5-11. Now make a copy of this submodel, as shown in Figure 5-17.

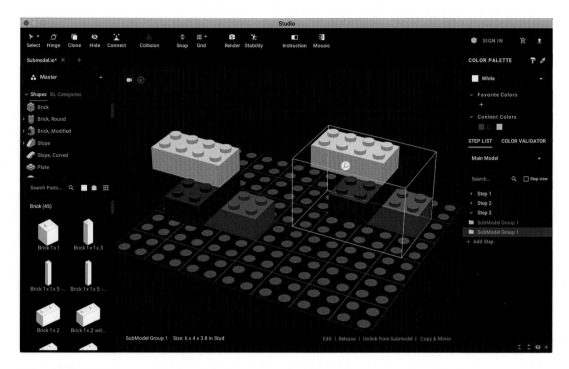

Figure 5-17. *Copy of submodel*

Now select one of the submodels. If you don't use the "Unlink from Submodel" option and click the "Edit" option available at the bottom of the user interface, then an alert window will appear which says "All linked submodels will be affected by this action," as shown in Figure 5-18. It means whatever changes you do in any of the submodels will reflect on all other submodels.

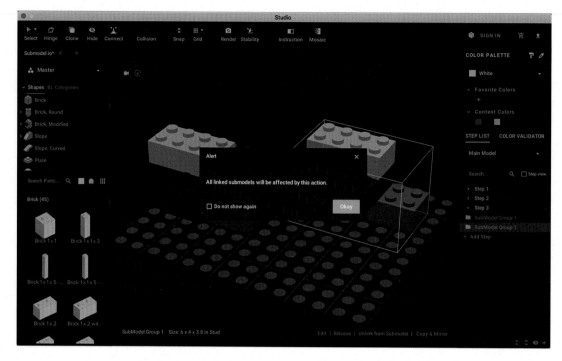

Figure 5-18. *Linked submodels*

If you select okay in the alert window, as shown in Figure 5-18, then the Studio will make all other models transparent except the submodel you chose to edit, as shown in Figure 5-19.

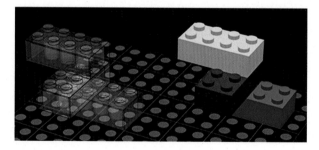

Figure 5-19. *Editing one of the linked submodels*

After that, I added one 2*4 brick to one of the linked submodels. While adding a 2*4 brick, you can see a transparent 2*4 brick also added automatically to other linked submodels, as shown in Figure 5-20.

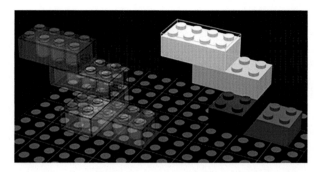

Figure 5-20. *Adding one 2*4 brick to one of the linked submodels*

After required changes in the submodel, you can go back to the main model by clicking the "Return to main model" option available at the bottom of the user interface, as shown in Figure 5-21. After returning to the main model, all the submodels will be visible in the normal form, as shown in Figure 5-22.

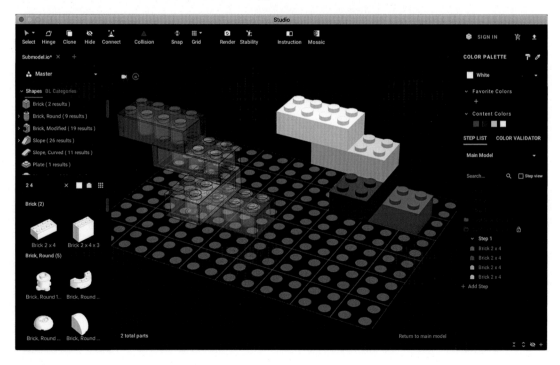

Figure 5-21. *Return to main model*

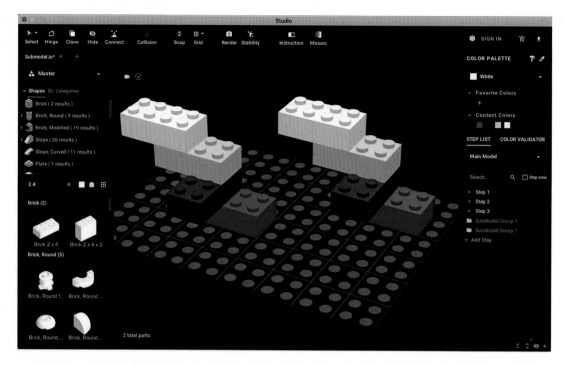

Figure 5-22. *Main model*

Copy and Mirror

Copy and Mirror option is a little different than the clone tool. The clone tool creates a copy of a particular submodel or a part. But Copy and Mirror will give you a mirrored copy of a submodel or a part.

I have created a submodel using three 2*4 bricks, as shown in Figure 5-23.

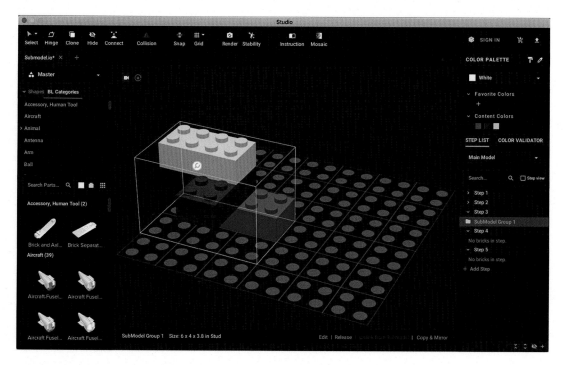

Figure 5-23. *A submodel*

After that, I clicked the Copy and Mirror option available at the bottom of the user interface, as shown in Figure 5-24. After that, it gave a mirrored copy of the submodel.

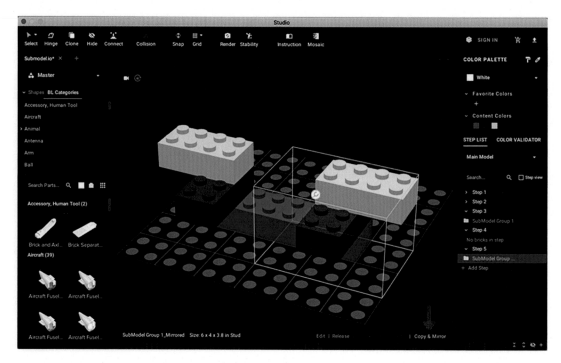

Figure 5-24. *Mirrored copy of a submodel*

The Studio will always make the mirrored copy of the part on the right side of the selected part.

Part Number, Name, Price, and Size

When you select any part on the building plate, the Studio will show its part number, name, price, and size at the bottom of the user interface.

I have selected a 2*4 brick on the building plate. See all the details of this part marked in red rectangle, as shown in Figure 5-25.

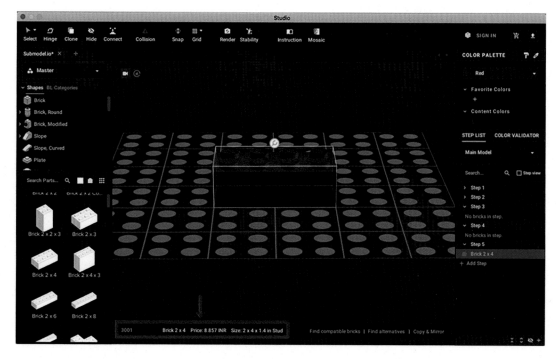

Figure 5-25. *Part no., name, price, and size*

The first thing you will see is part number which is 3001 for 2*4 brick. You can also click on this part no. and it will open the bricklink website with more details of the part, as shown in Figure 5-26.

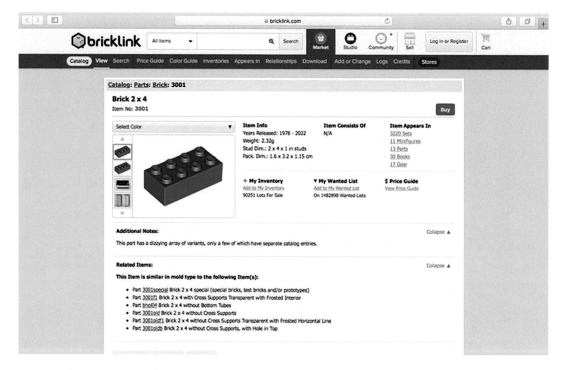

Figure 5-26. *Part information on Bricklink.com*

Then it will show the part name, which is 2*4 brick, as shown in Figure 5-25.

After the part name, it will show the price. The price of one 2*4 red brick is 8.854 INR, as shown in Figure 5-25.

And last, it will show you the size of the part. The size of the 2*4 brick is 2*4*1.4 in the stud, as shown in Figure 5-25.

When you select the multiple bricks, the Studio will show you only how many parts you have selected, the price of selected parts altogether, and the size of the selected parts based on the area it is covering in studs, as shown in Figure 5-27.

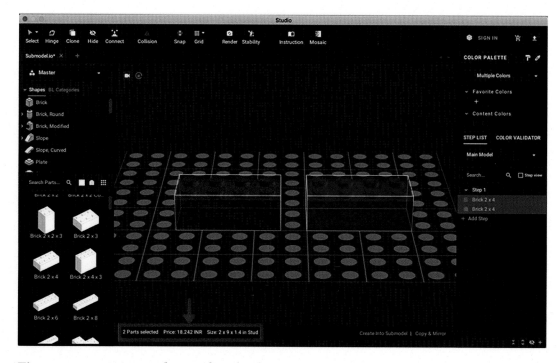

Figure 5-27. *Price and size of multiple selected parts*

Conclusion

In this chapter, you learned about different design tools, that is, Find Compatible Bricks, Find Alternatives, Copy and Mirror, Create into Submodel, Part no., Type, Price, and Size. These tools are very useful when you are designing any model.

In the next chapter, you will learn about the step list and color validator.

CHAPTER 6

Step List and Color Validator

In this chapter, I will explain about step list and color validator in detail, which is situated in the right corner of the software, as shown in Figure 6-1.

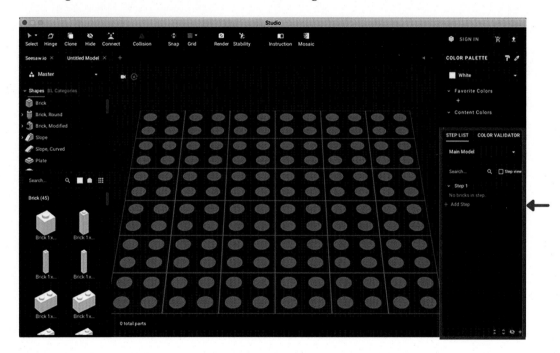

Figure 6-1. *Step list and color validator*

Step List and Color Validator options are very useful to create and manage steps of your model.

I have created a model of a seesaw, as shown in Figure 6-2. I will take the reference of this model to explain the different options available in the step list and color validator.

© Vishnu Agarwal 2023
V. Agarwal, *The Art of Virtual LEGO Design*, https://doi.org/10.1007/978-1-4842-8777-4_6

Figure 6-2. *Seesaw model*

Add, Delete, Shift, and Describe Step

- **Add a step**

To add a new step, you need to click the "Add Step" option available at the end of steps section, as shown in Figure 6-3.

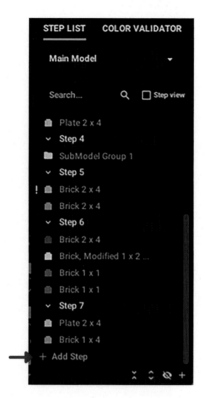

Figure 6-3. *Adding a new step*

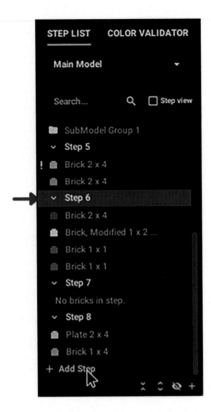

Figure 6-4. *Adding a new step while another step is selected*

Figure 6-5. *Adding a new step while another part is selected*

While adding a new step if you have selected any step, then a new step will be added after that selected step. For example, as shown in Figure 6-4, I selected step 6 and then added a step so a new step was added after step 6 which is step 7 and not at the end.

And while adding a new step if you have selected any part, then a new step will be added at the end of all the steps. For example, as shown in Figure 6-5, I selected a part brick 1*1 and then added a step so a new step was added at the end which is step 9.

- **Delete a step**

If you want to delete a step, then select that step and click the delete option available next to step no., or right-click the mouse on that step and select the delete option, as shown in Figures 6-6 and 6-7.

When you delete the very first step, then the parts of that step will be shifted to the next available step, and if you delete any other step, then the parts of that step will shift to the previous available step.

- **Shift a step**

If you want to shift a step before or after any step, then you need to select the step which you want to shift, left-click the mouse, hold, and drag to the desired location and release the left button.

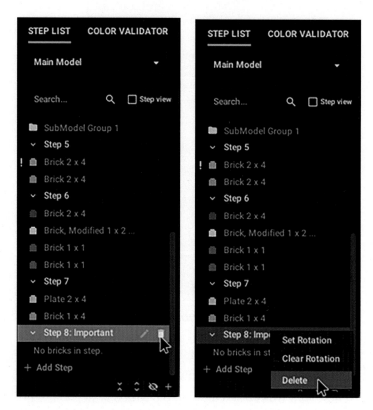

Figures 6-6 and 6-7. *Deleting a step*

As shown in Figures 6-8, 6-9, and 6-10, I have shifted step 7 (last step) before step 6. After shifting, step 7 became step 6 and vice versa and all the parts associated with that step will also shift along with the step.

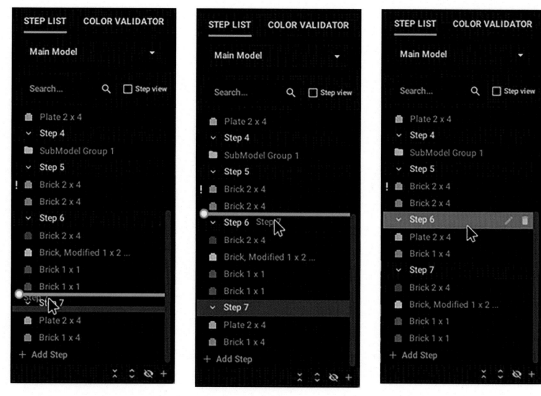

Figures 6-8, 6-9, and 6-10. *Shifting a step*

- **Step description**

To add a description in the step, you need to click the Edit option, as shown in Figure 6-11. After that, a new window will appear where you can write the description of the step, as shown in Figure 6-12. Once you finish writing the description click Okay. The description will be visible next to the step no., as shown in Figure 6-13.

Figure 6-11. *Edit option*

Figure 6-12. *Description window*

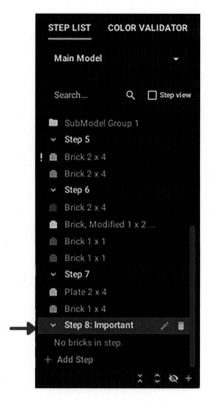

Figure 6-13. *After adding description*

Add, Hide, Delete, and Shift a Part

- **Add a part**

While building, the model parts will automatically be added inside the first step. Otherwise, you need to create the steps to add parts in different steps as needed and as shown in Figure 6-14.

Figure 6-14. *Adding parts inside steps*

- **Hide a part**

When you hover the mouse pointer on the part, then the hide option will be visible, as shown in Figure 6-15. Once you click the hidden symbol, it will be highlighted, as shown in Figure 6-16, and that particular part will be hidden.

Figure 6-15. *Hide a part symbol*

Figure 6-16. *Highlighted hide part symbol*

In this particular case, I have hidden a 2*4 red brick. If you compare Figures 6-17 and 6-18, then you can see that in Figure 6-18 a 2*4 red brick is hidden.

After hiding the part(s), you can see in the top right corner the number of all the hidden parts will appear and once you click the "Show all" option, all the hidden parts will be visible again, as shown in Figure 6-18.

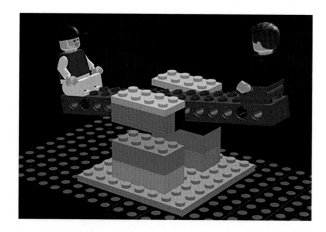

Figure 6-17. *Seesaw model before hiding a part*

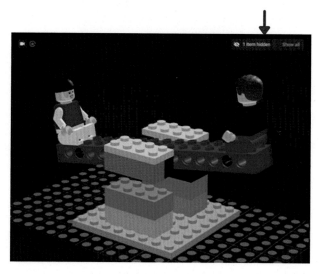

Figure 6-18. *Hidden 2*4 red brick in seesaw model*

- **Delete a part**

When you hover the mouse pointer on the part, then the delete option will be visible, as shown in Figure 6-19. Once you click the delete symbol, it will delete the part.

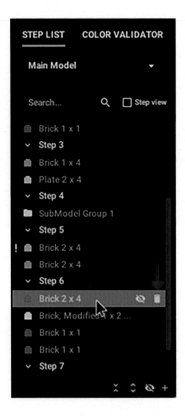

Figure 6-19. *Delete a part*

- **Shift a part**

If you want to shift a part in some other step, then you need to select the part which you want to shift, left-click the mouse, hold, and drag to the desired step and release the left button.

As shown in Figures 6-20, 6-21, and 6-22, I have shifted the part red brick 2*4 from step 6 to step 7. While shifting, you will see a blue line appearing which will help you to place the part at the correct location.

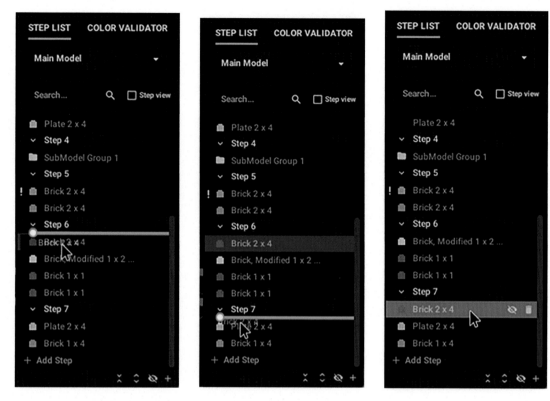

Figures 6-20, 6-21, and 6-22. *Shifting a part*

Another way to shift a part to some other step is to select the part (brick 2*4) which you want to shift, right-click the mouse and select the **MoveTo** option, as shown in Figure 6-23. After selecting the **MoveTo** option, you will get the option of **steps**, as shown in Figure 6-24. You can select the step where you want to shift the part. I have shifted the brick 2*4 from step 2 to step 3, as shown in Figure 6-25.

Figure 6-23. *Right-click a part*

Figure 6-24. *Selecting the step*

Figure 6-25. *Part moved to another step*

Expand and Collapse, Edit, Hide, and Delete Submodel

When you create a submodel, that will be a part of the step. When you hover your mouse pointer on the submodel, you will get Expand, Edit, Hide, and Delete options, as shown in Figure 6-26.

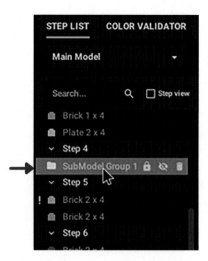

Figure 6-26. *Submodel options*

- **Expand and collapse submodel**

To expand the submodel you need to click the folder symbol available at the start of the submodel part, as shown in Figure 6-27. When it expands, you can see all the steps associated with that submodel in the light color, which means you can only see those steps but cannot edit.

Figure 6-27. *Expand and collapse submodel*

You can collapse the submodel by clicking the same folder symbol.

- **Edit the submodel**

To edit the steps and parts of the submodel, you need to click the Edit option, as shown in Figure 6-28. Once you click the Edit option, it will open all the steps and parts associated with that submodel in the editable format. Now you can edit the steps and parts of the submodel as needed and as shown in Figure 6-29.

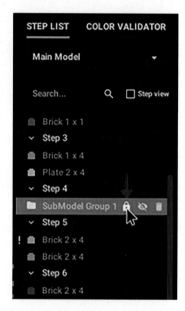

Figure 6-28. *Edit option for the submodel*

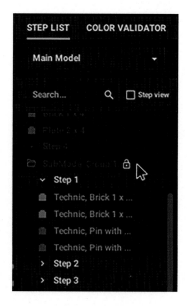

Figure 6-29. *Steps associated with the submodel*

- **Hide the submodel**

When you hover the mouse pointer on the submodel, then the hide option will be visible, as shown in Figure 6-30. Once you click the hidden symbol, it will be highlighted, as shown in Figure 6-31, and that particular submodel will be hidden.

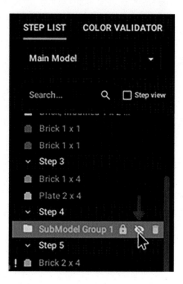

Figure 6-30. *Hide the submodel*

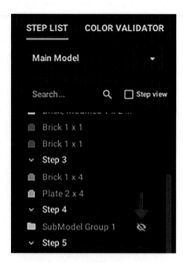

Figure 6-31. *Highlighted hide submodel symbol*

- **Delete the submodel**

When you hover the mouse pointer on the submodel, then the delete option will be visible, as shown in Figure 6-32. Once you click the delete symbol, it will delete the submodel.

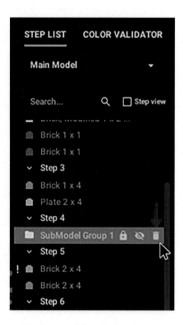

Figure 6-32. *Delete the submodel*

Expand and Collapse Steps

You can click the arrow symbol situated before each step to expand and collapse the steps, as shown in Figure 6-33. After expanding the step, you can see all the parts associated with that step.

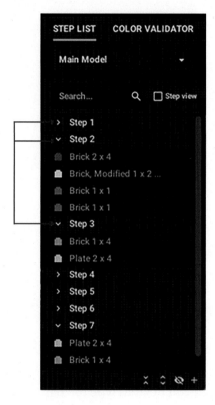

Figure 6-33. *Expand and collapse option*

Model Dropdown Menu

The model dropdown menu is situated at the top of the step list section, as shown in Figure 6-34. When you click that, it will show you the main model and all the submodels created in the main model.

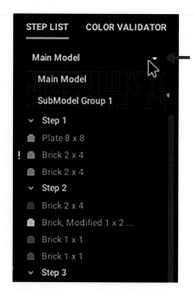

Figure 6-34. *Model dropdown menu*

Using the model dropdown menu you can easily select the submodels and do the required modifications if needed.

Search in the Step List

The search box in the step list is situated below the model dropdown menu, as shown in Figure 6-35. This search box is used to find any part in the steps. For example, if you have to search 2*4 bricks, then you need to type the part name and you can see all the 2*4 bricks available in the steps, as shown in Figure 6-36.

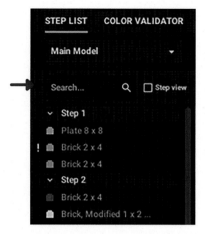

Figure 6-35. *Search box in step list*

Figure 6-36. *Searching 2*4 bricks in steps*

Step List Tools

The step list tools are available at the bottom of the step list section, as shown in
Figure 6-37.

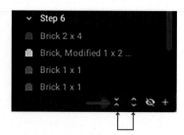

Figure 6-37. *Collapse and expand steps*

You can click the arrow symbols, as shown in Figure 6-37, to expand and collapse the steps. After expanding the step you can see all the parts associated with that step.

You can use the hide option to hide any part(s), as shown in Figure 6-38. If you select a part and click the hide option, then only that part will be hidden, but if you select a step and click on the hide option, then all the parts associated with that step will be hidden.

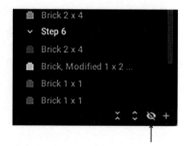

Figure 6-38. *Hide the parts*

You can use the "Add a Step" option to add a new step, as shown in Figure 6-39. While adding a new step, if you have selected any step, then a new step will be added after that selected step, and while adding a new step, if you have selected any part, then a new step will be added at the end of all the steps.

Figure 6-39. *Add a step*

Step View

The **Step view** is situated next to the search box in the step list. To activate the step view mode, you need to select the check box, as shown in Figure 6-40.

Figure 6-40. *Activate the step view*

The step view can be used for

- Previewing up to a chosen step.

- Setting the camera rotation of the step.

- Clearing the camera rotation of the step.

- **Preview up to a chosen step**

After activating the step view, you can click the steps to see the preview up to a chosen step. For example, when you click step 1, it will show the preview of all the parts available in step 1 and hide all other steps, as shown in Figure 6-41. Similarly, when you select steps 2 and 3, Studio will preview the steps up to steps 2 and 3, respectively, as shown in Figure 6-42 and Figure 6-43.

Figure 6-41. *Preview upto step 1*

Figure 6-42. *Preview upto step 2*

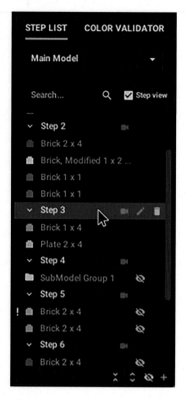

Figure 6-43. *Preview upto step 3*

This feature of the Studio is helpful to check the flow of steps and create the building instruction. In case any modifications are required, then you can do it very easily using step view.

- **Set the camera rotation of the step**

Another feature of the step view is to set the camera rotation of the steps. The first way to set the camera rotation is by using the camera button. First, you need to set the view of the step manually or use viewport controls (Chapter 1). Once you finish setting the camera angle, you need to click the camera button, as shown in Figure 6-44.

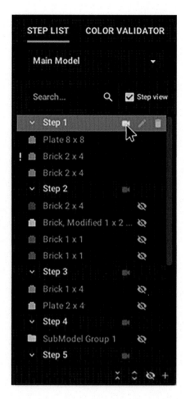

Figure 6-44. *Set the camera rotation using camera button*

The second way to set the camera rotation is by right-clicking the step and selecting the "Set Rotation" option, as shown in Figure 6-45. After that, it will open a new window called "Set Camera Rotation," as shown in Figure 6-46. You can set the camera rotation by selecting the angles from the preset dropdown menu or you can type your own values for X and Y angles.

Figure 6-45. *Set the camera rotation by right clicking the step*

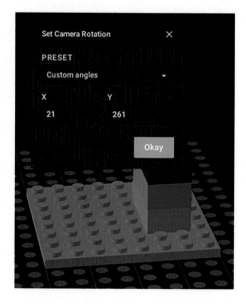

Figure 6-46. *Camera rotation angles*

Using viewport controls, I have set the camera rotation for each step of the seesaw model in step view mode. You can see all the different camera rotations for steps in Figures 6-47 to 6-52.

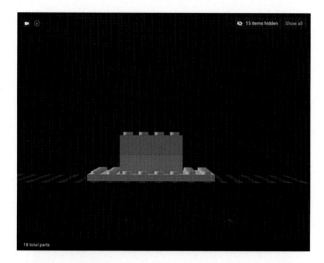

Figure 6-47. *Step 1: Front view*

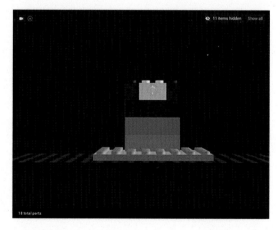

Figure 6-48. *Step 2: Back view*

Figure 6-49. *Step 3: Left view*

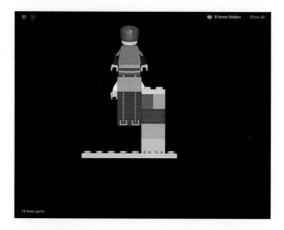

Figure 6-50. *Step 4: Right view*

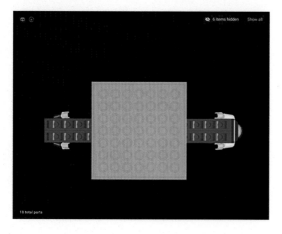

Figure 6-51. *Step 5: Bottom view*

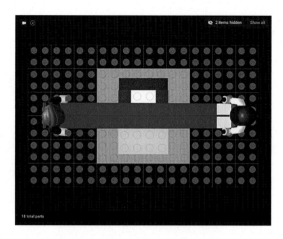

Figure 6-52. *Step 6: Top view*

- **Clear the camera rotation of the step**

If you need to delete or modify the camera rotation for the step, you first need to clear the camera rotation. To remove the camera rotation, you need to right-click the step and you will get the option to clear the camera rotation. You need to click "Clear Rotation" to delete the camera rotation of the step, as shown in Figure 6-53.

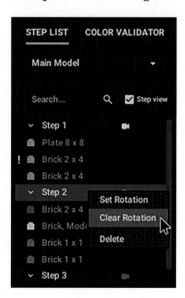

Figure 6-53. *Clear the camera rotation*

Color Validator

The color validator is used to fix the problems of unavailable part colors in your model. When you see an exclamation mark with any part in the step list, then it means the selected color is unavailable for that part.

Glow in dark purple color is unavailable for 2*4 brick in step 1, as shown in Figure 6-54, and glow in dark orange is unavailable for 2*4 brick in step 5, as shown in Figure 6-55. In both cases, you can see the exclamation mark in the parts.

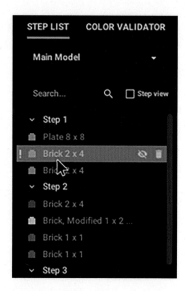

Figure 6-54. *Color unavailable in step 1*

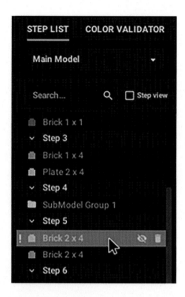

Figure 6-55. *Color unavailable in step 2*

Now let's understand how you will fix this unavailable color problem.

You need to select the **color validator** option available next to step list, as shown in Figure 6-56. Here you will see all the parts with unavailable colors.

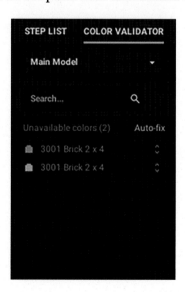

Figure 6-56. *Color validator option*

The first way to fix the problem of unavailable color is to click on the **Auto fix** option, as shown in Figure 6-57. Once you click the Auto-fix option, it will change all the unavailable colors to the nearest available color and all the unavailable color parts will disappear from the color validator list, as shown in Figure 6-58.

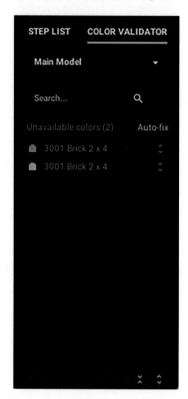

Figure 6-57. *Auto-fix option*

Figure 6-58. *After auto fixing the unavailable colors*

Before applying the Auto-fix, the unavailable colors for 2*4 bricks were **Glow in dark orange** and **Glow in dark purple,** as shown in Figure 6-59, and after applying the auto-fix the unavailable colors changed to **Metallic gold** and **Medium lavender,** as shown in Figure 6-60.

Figure 6-59. *Before Auto-fix*

Figure 6-60. *After Auto-fix*

Another way to fix the problem of unavailable colors is to replace the colors manually. You need to select each unavailable color manually in the color validator list to replace it with another color.

As shown in Figure 6-61, I selected the glow-in-dark orange color in the color validator list which is the unavailable color. After selecting the unavailable color, it opened the options for replacement color. You can change the color by opening the drop-down menu of the replacement color. Also, when you select this unavailable color, it will highlight that part in the seesaw model and the other parts will become translucent.

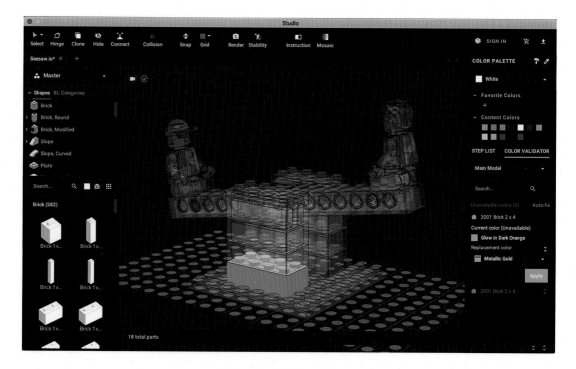

Figure 6-61. *Manual-fixing of unavailable colors*

Similarly, you can select other unavailable colors in the color validator list and replace the unavailable colors with the other available colors.

Once you replace all the unavailable colors with some other color, then all the unavailable color parts will disappear from the color validator list, as shown in Figure 6-62.

Figure 6-62. *After manual-fixing of unavailable colors*

Conclusion

I tried my best to explain all the options available in the step list and color validator. While building a model step list, color validator plays a very important role.

In the next chapter, you will learn about render and stability tools.

CHAPTER 7

Render and Stability

In this chapter, I will explain render and stability tools in detail, which are situated at the top of the Studio user interface, as shown in Figure 7-1. I will use one of the most famous LEGO duck models to demonstrate the render and stability tools.

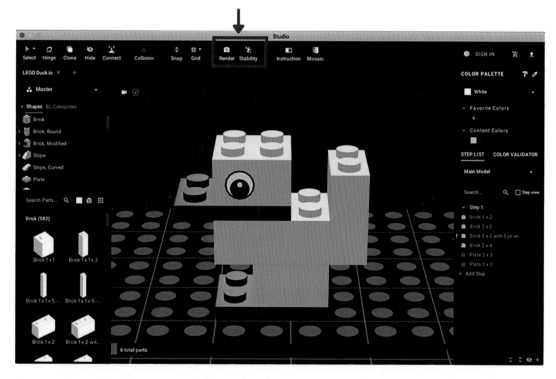

Figure 7-1. *Render and stability tools*

Render and stability tools are used post-completion of your model.

© Vishnu Agarwal 2023
V. Agarwal, *The Art of Virtual LEGO Design*, https://doi.org/10.1007/978-1-4842-8777-4_7

Render

When you click the render option, as shown in Figure 7-1, then a new window will open, as shown in Figure 7-2. To understand each part of the render window, I have divided it into seven sections:

- A. Preview

- B. Photoreal

- C. POV-Ray

- D. Animation

- E. Close the dialog on starting rendering

- F. Format

- G. Queue

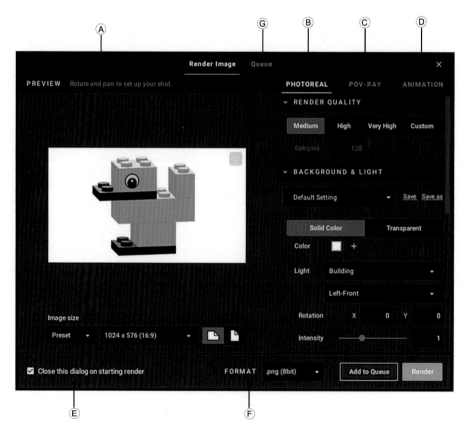

Figure 7-2. Render window

A. Preview

The white rectangle window shown in Figure 7-3 is the place where you can rotate and pan your model to set up your shot before rendering. You can align the object present in the preview window to the camera center by pressing the button as pointed by the red arrow.

Figure 7-3. *Preview*

You can also set the image size by selecting the options from the dropdown menu available under the preview window as shown in Figure 7-3. You can select the image sizes available in the preset option or you can also customize the size. It also gives you the option to set the image to landscape or portrait.

B. Photoreal

There are two types of render engines through which you can render the LEGO model image. The first one is Photoreal. Photorealistic rendering is a type of 3D rendering where the final result is very difficult to distinguish from a photograph of a real-life LEGO model.

- **Render Quality**

The first setting in the photoreal is **render quality**. You can select the options from medium, high, very high, and custom, based on your requirement, as shown in

Figure 7-4. As you increase the quality, the sample rate of the image will increase and the time taken to render the image will also increase.

Figure 7-4. *Photoreal render quality*

- **Background and Light**

The second setting in the photoreal is the background and light.

You can select the background as solid or transparent. When you select the solid color background, then you can change the background color by clicking the color tab, as shown in Figure 7-5. You can also add your favorite background colors by clicking the "+" symbol.

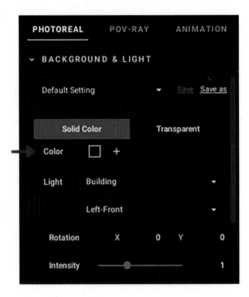

Figure 7-5. *Photoreal solid color background*

When you select the transparent background, you will get the floor shadow option, as shown in Figure 7-6. If you want the model floor shadow then select the checkbox or else unselect the checkbox.

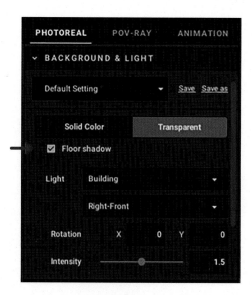

Figure 7-6. *Photoreal transparent background*

You can control the type and position of the light source by selecting the options from the two dropdown menus under the light section, as shown in Figure 7-7.

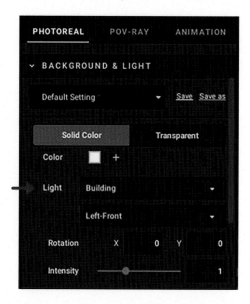

Figure 7-7. *Photoreal light source type and direction*

The first dropdown menu under the light section is for the light source type and the second is for the light source position.

Under solid color background, you will get two options for light source type, that is, building and mechanic. And under the transparent background, you will get five options for light source type, that is, building, mechanic, asteroid, dawn, and piazza.

For both solid and transparent backgrounds, there are four options for light source position, that is, left-front, right-front, left-rear, and right-rear, as shown in Figure 7-8. The light source position means from where the light is coming and projecting on the model.

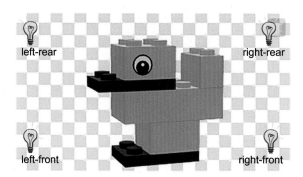

Figure 7-8. *Different light source positions*

You can control the light source rotation by changing the values of the X and Y axes. You can also change the light intensity by moving the slider button or by directly typing the value, as shown in Figure 7-9.

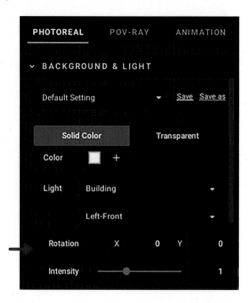

Figure 7-9. *Photoreal light source rotation and intensity*

The minimum value for intensity is 0 and the maximum is 3.

After adjusting all the settings of the background and light, you can save the settings as your default settings, as shown in Figure 7-10.

Figure 7-10. *Photoreal background and light default setting*

You can also save the settings as your new custom preset. When you click on the "Save as" option, as shown in Figure 7-10, one new window will open where you can choose the name of your new custom preset, as shown in Figure 7-11.

Figure 7-11. *Adding a new custom preset*

After adding a new default setting, if you want to delete that setting option, then you need to click the dropdown menu of the default setting and click the delete option present next to the default setting, as shown in Figure 7-12.

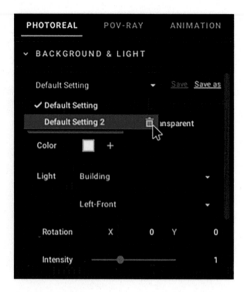

Figure 7-12. *Deleting a custom preset*

When you are deleting any custom preset under the default setting dropdown menu, then you need to make sure that you have not selected that custom preset as your current setting. Otherwise, you will not see the option to delete that custom preset.

- **Camera setup**

The third setting in the photoreal is the camera setup.

You can set the camera position as the **perspective view** or **orthographic view**, as shown in Figure 7-13.

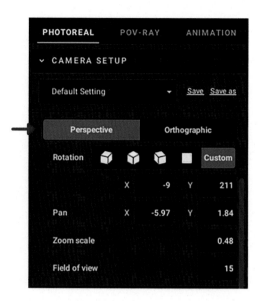

Figure 7-13. *Perspective and orthographic camera view*

The **perspective view** is the art of representing three-dimensional objects on a two-dimensional surface so as to give the right impression of their height, width, depth, and position in relation to each other.

An **orthographic view** is a two-dimensional view of a three-dimensional object. An orthographic view is created by projecting a view of an object onto a plane which is usually positioned so that it is parallel to one of the planes of the object.

You can select the camera rotation from four preset options or select the custom option to change manually, as shown in Figure 7-14.

You can use the right button on your mouse to rotate the camera view of the model in the preview window or directly type the X and Y axes values to rotate, as shown in Figure 7-14.

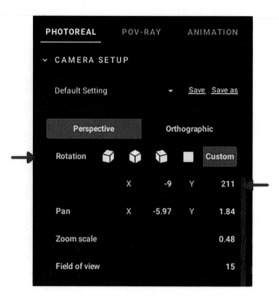

Figure 7-14. *Camera rotation*

When you use the right button on your mouse to rotate the camera view of the model in the preview window, then the X-axis rotation will change in the up and down direction and the Y-axis rotation will change in right and left direction, as shown in Figure 7-15.

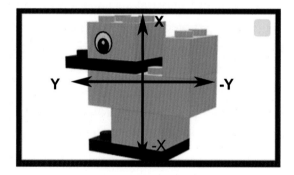

Figure 7-15. *Camera rotation in X and Y axes*

You can use the left button on your mouse to pan the camera view of the model in the preview window or directly type the X and Y axes values to pan, as shown in Figure 7-16.

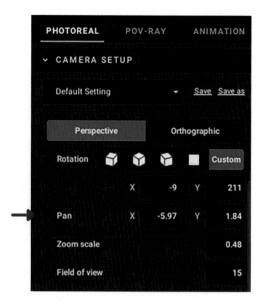

Figure 7-16. *Camera pan*

When you use the left button on your mouse to pan the camera view of the model in the preview window, then the X-axis will change in the right and left direction and the Y-axis will change in the up and down direction, as shown in Figure 7-17.

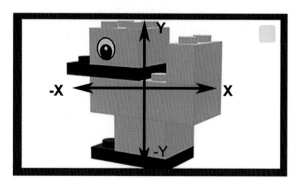

Figure 7-17. *Camera pan in X and Y axes*

Panning means swiveling a still or video camera horizontally from a fixed position. This motion is similar to the motion of a person when they turn their head on their neck from left to right.

You can use the center scroll wheel on your mouse to control the zoom scale by moving up and down, as shown in Figure 7-18.

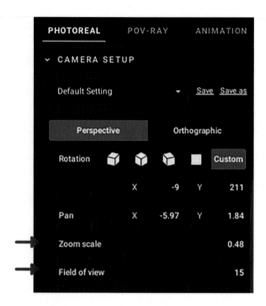

Figure 7-18. *Zoom scale and field of view*

You can also change the field of view by directly typing the value in the number box, as shown in Figure 7-18. Field of view is defined as how far or near the camera is situated from the model.

Different values of the field of view will also affect the pan and zoom scale behavior. Try to play with the different values of the field of view and change the pan and zoom scale to understand it better.

After adjusting all the settings of the camera setup, you can save the settings as your default settings, as shown in Figure 7-19.

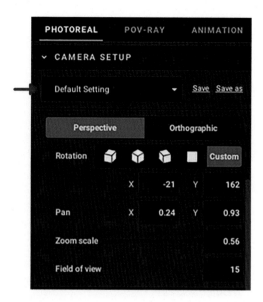

Figure 7-19. *Photoreal camera setup default setting*

You can also save the settings as your new custom preset. When you click on the "Save as" option, as shown in Figure 7-19, one new window will open where you can choose the name of your new custom preset, as shown in Figure 7-20.

Figure 7-20. *Adding a new custom preset*

After adding a new default setting, if you want to delete that setting option, then you need to click on the dropdown menu of the default setting and click the delete option present next to the default setting, as shown in Figure 7-21.

Figure 7-21. *Deleting a custom preset*

When you are deleting any custom preset under the default setting dropdown menu, then you need to make sure that you have not selected that custom preset as your current setting. Otherwise, you will not see the option to delete that custom preset.

- **Material effects**

The fourth and last setting in the photoreal is the material effects. You can turn ON and OFF the stud logo, UV degradation, and scratches as shown in Figure 7-22.

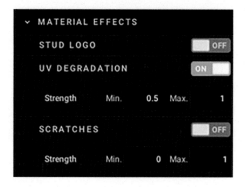

Figure 7-22. *Material effects*

If you want the LEGO name to be printed on the bricks after rendering, then turn ON this option or else turn OFF as shown in Figures 7-23 and 7-24.

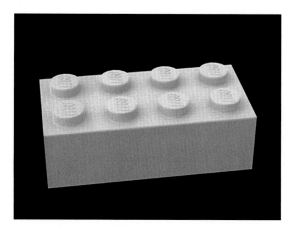

Figure 7-23. *With stud logo*

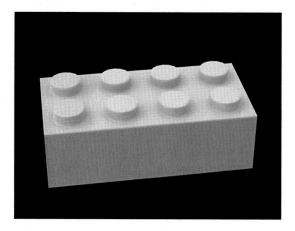

Figure 7-24. *Without stud logo*

UV degradation refers to the cracking or disintegration of materials exposed to ultraviolet radiation, most commonly due to sunlight exposure.

You can turn ON and OFF the UV degradation effect, as shown in Figure 7-22. If the UV degradation effect is turned ON then it will give you the effect as the brick has been exposed to sunlight after rendering the image, as shown in Figure 7-25. You can compare the UV degraded LEGO 2*4 brick with the strength of a minimum of 0.5 and a maximum of 1, as shown in Figure 7-25, with the without UV degraded LEGO 2*4 brick, as shown in Figure 7-26.

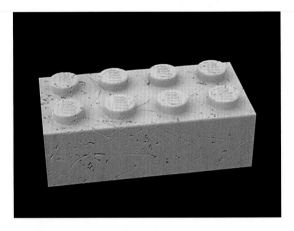

Figure 7-25. *With UV degradation*

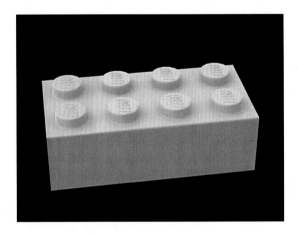

Figure 7-26. *Without UV degradation*

You can control the strength of the UV degradation by typing the minimum (0) and maximum (1) values, as shown in Figure 7-22.

Scratches refer to the marks or abrasions on the surface of LEGO parts.

You can turn ON and OFF the scratches effect, as shown in Figure 7-22. You can compare the scratched LEGO 2*4 brick with the strength of a minimum of 0.5 and a maximum of 1, as shown in Figure 7-27, with the without scratched LEGO 2*4 brick, as shown in Figure 7-28.

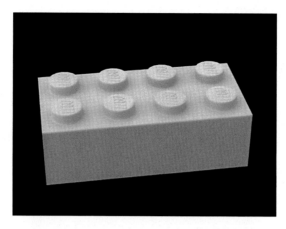

Figure 7-27. *With scratches*

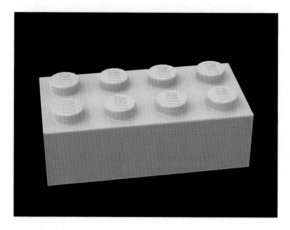

Figure 7-28. *Without scratches*

You can control the strength of scratches by typing the minimum (0) and maximum (1) values, as shown in Figure 7-22.

C. POV-Ray

The second type of render engine is POV-Ray through which you can render the LEGO model image. POV-Ray is the acronym of the Persistence of Vision Ray Tracer.

- **Render Quality**

The first setting in the POV-Ray is **render quality**. You can select the options from low, medium, high, and custom, based on your requirement, as shown in Figure 7-29. As you change the render quality, the other options like **use high-quality model, stud logo, shadow quality, and max trace level** will change automatically. But if you choose custom, you can change these options as you want.

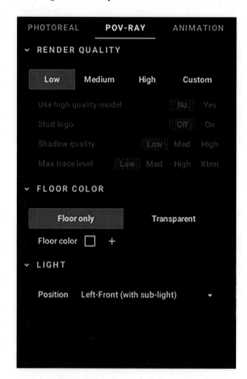

Figure 7-29. *POV-Ray render quality*

- **Floor Color**

The second setting in the POV-Ray is the floor color.

You can select the background as floor only or transparent. When you select the floor-only background, then you can change the background color by clicking the color tab, as shown in Figure 7-30. You can also add your favorite background colors by clicking the "+" symbol.

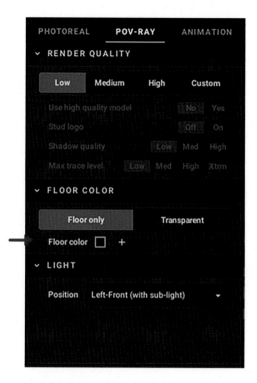

Figure 7-30. *POV-Ray floor only background*

When you select the transparent background, you will not get the floor shadow option like the photoreal render engine, as shown in Figure 7-31. You can only render a transparent image of your LEGO model.

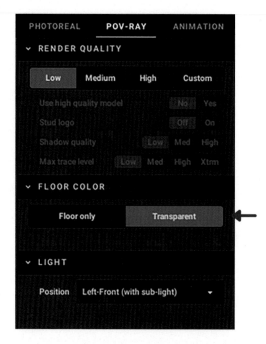

Figure 7-31. *POV-Ray transparent background Light*

- **Light**

The third and last setting in the POV-Ray is the light.

You can control the position of the light source by selecting the options from the position dropdown menu, as shown in Figure 7-32.

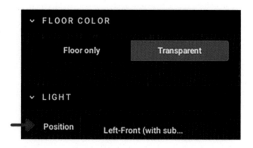

Figure 7-32. *POV-Ray light source position*

When you click on the position dropdown menu, then you will get ten different options, that is, left-front (with sub-light), left, right, right back, etc.

As example of the light source, which is situated on the left, is shown in Figure 7-33. The light source position means from where the light is coming and projecting on the model.

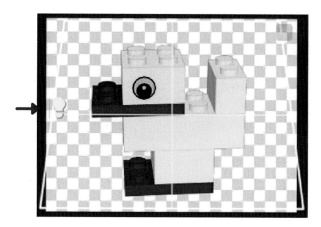

Figure 7-33. *Light source position: Left*

DIFFERENCE BETWEEN PHOTOREAL AND POV-RAY RENDERED IMAGES

You can see the clear difference between the photoreal rendered image as shown in Figure 7-34 and the POV-Ray rendered image as shown in Figure 7-35. Photoreal render engine gives you a more realistic view compared to POV-Ray.

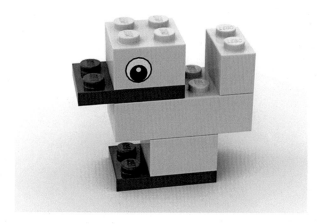

Figure 7-34. *Photoreal rendered image*

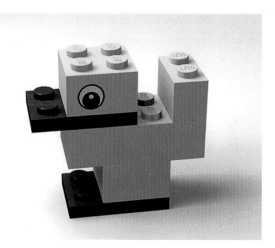

Figure 7-35. *POV-Ray rendered image*

D. Animation

This is one of the most amazing features of Studio 2.0. You can animate your model by giving some effects like building sequence, bricks falling down, and revolving.

- **Quality**

The first setting in the animation is quality, as shown in Figure 7-36.

Figure 7-36. *Frame rate and duration*

Under quality, you can select the **fps** as 1, 24, 30, or 60, as shown in Figure 7-36. FPS is the abbreviation for **frames per second**. It is used to measure the number of still image frames in a per-second video. The higher the fps, the smoother the motion of animation.

You can also set the duration of the animation by typing the number of seconds, as shown in Figure 7-36.

- **Effects**

The second setting in the animation is effects, as shown in Figure 7-37.

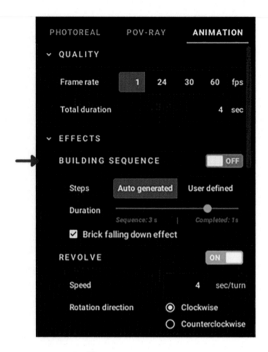

Figure 7-37. *Building sequence effect*

You can create a building sequence effect by turning ON this setting, as shown in Figure 7-37. The building sequence steps could be auto-generated by the Studio or you can select user-defined. User-defined steps will follow the same building sequence in which you created the building instructions.

You can set the building sequence duration using the slider button, and while generating the building sequence if you also want to add a brick falling down effect, then select the check box present under the duration, or else unselect the check box, as shown in Figure 7-37.

Another effect that you can create in your animation is revolving. Turn ON the revolve option if you want to add this effect, as shown in Figure 7-38. You can also control the speed of revolving by typing the value in the number box.

Figure 7-38. *Revolving effect*

And last, you can select the revolve direction as clockwise or counterclockwise, as shown in Figure 7-38.

- **Render Quality**

The third setting in the animation is **render quality**. You can select the options from medium, high, very high, and custom based on your requirement, as shown in Figure 7-39. As you increase the quality, the sample rate of the image will increase and the time taken to render the image will also increase.

Figure 7-39. *Animation render quality*

- **Background and Light**

The fourth setting in the animation is the background and light.

You can change the background color of the model by clicking the color tab, as shown in Figure 7-40. You can also add your favorite background colors by clicking the "+" symbol.

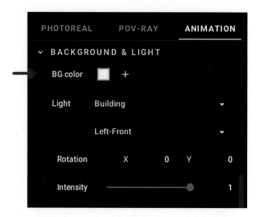

Figure 7-40. *Animation background color*

You can control the type and position of the light source by selecting the options from the two dropdown menus under the Light section, as shown in Figure 7-41.

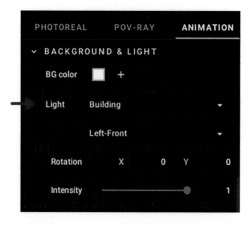

Figure 7-41. *Animation light source type and direction*

The first dropdown menu under the Light section is for the light source type and the second is for the light source position.

You will get two options for light source type, that is, building and mechanic, and four options for light source position, that is, left-front, right-front, left-rear, and right-rear, as shown in Figure 7-42. The light source position means from where the light is coming and projecting on the model.

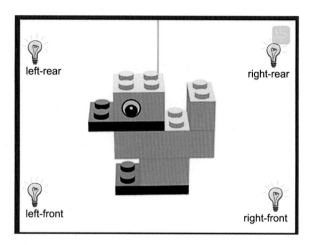

Figure 7-42. *Different light source positions*

You can control the light source rotation by changing the values of the X and Y axes. You can also change the light intensity by moving the slider button or by directly typing the value, as shown in Figure 7-43.

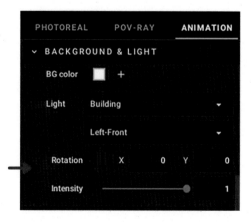

Figure 7-43. *Animation light source rotation and intensity*

The minimum value for intensity is 0 and the maximum is 1.

- **Camera setup**

The fifth setting in the animation is the camera setup.

You can select the camera rotation from four preset options or select the custom option to change manually, as shown in Figure 7-44.

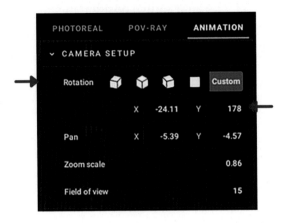

Figure 7-44. *Animation camera rotation*

You can use the right button on your mouse to rotate the camera view of the model in the preview window or directly type the X and Y axes values to rotate, as shown in Figure 7-44.

When you use the right button on your mouse to rotate the camera view of the model in the preview window, then the X-axis rotation will change in the up and down direction and the Y-axis rotation will change in right and left direction, as shown in Figure 7-45.

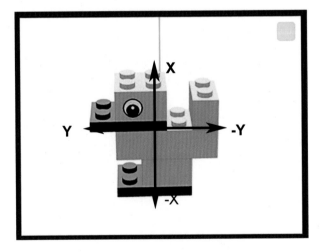

Figure 7-45. *Camera rotation in X and Y axes*

You can use the left button on your mouse to pan the camera view of the model in the preview window or directly type the X and Y axes values to pan, as shown in Figure 7-46.

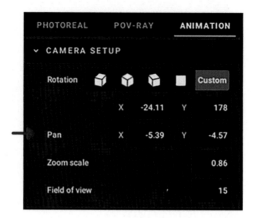

Figure 7-46. *Camera pan*

When you use the left button on your mouse to pan the camera view of the model in the preview window, then the X-axis will change in the right and left direction and the Y-axis will change in the up and down direction, as shown in Figure 7-47.

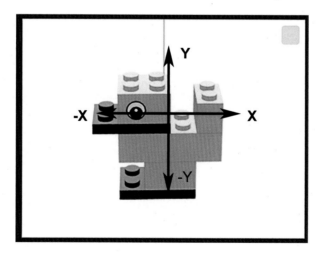

Figure 7-47. *Camera pan in X and Y axes*

Panning means swiveling a still or video camera horizontally from a fixed position. This motion is similar to the motion of a person when they turn their head on their neck from left to right.

You can use the center scroll wheel on your mouse to control the zoom scale by moving up and down, as shown in Figure 7-48.

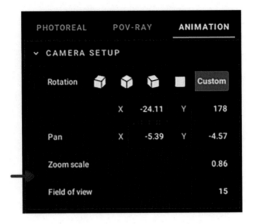

Figure 7-48. *Zoom scale and field of view*

You can also change the field of view by directly typing the value in the number box, as shown in Figure 7-48. Field of view is defined as how far or near the camera is situated from the model.

Different values of the field of view will also affect the pan and zoom scale behavior. Try to play with the different values of the field of view and change the pan and zoom scale to understand it better.

CAMERA CENTER FOR ANIMATION

The azure color line shown in the followingpreview window images is the camera center. When you animate your model and add the revolving effect, then the model will revolve through the center line only (this line won't be visible after rendering).

You can see the center line coming out from the top of the object, as shown in Figure 7-49. The bottom view of the center line is shown in Figure 7-50. I have moved the object to the right side of the center line, as shown in Figure 7-51. Now the object will revolve around this center line if you add a revolving effect in animation.

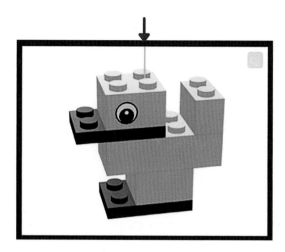

Figure 7-49. *Object at the camera center line*

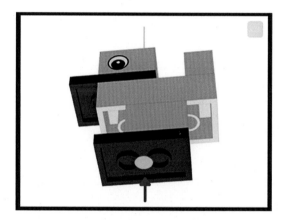

Figure 7-50. *Object at the camera center line bottom view*

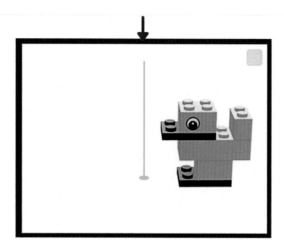

Figure 7-51. *Object at the right side of camera center line*

- **Material effects**

The sixth and last setting in the animation is the material effects. You can turn ON and OFF the stud logo, UV degradation, and scratches, as shown in Figure 7-52.

Figure 7-52. *Material effects*

If you want the LEGO name to be printed on the bricks after rendering, then turn ON this option or else turn OFF, as shown in Figures 7-53 and 7-54.

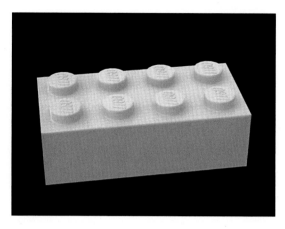

Figure 7-53. *With stud logo*

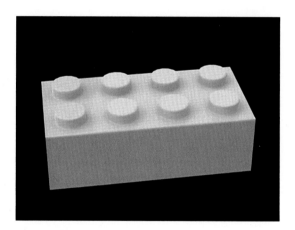

Figure 7-54. *Without stud logo*

UV degradation refers to the cracking or disintegration of materials exposed to ultraviolet radiation, most commonly due to sunlight exposure.

You can turn ON and OFF the UV degradation effect, as shown in Figure 7-52. If the UV degradation effect is turned ON, then it will give the effect as if the brick has been exposed to sunlight after rendering the image, as shown in Figure 7-55. You can compare the UV degraded LEGO 2*4 brick with the strength of a minimum of 0.5 and a maximum of 1 as shown in Figure 7-55 with the without UV degraded LEGO 2*4 brick, as shown in Figure 7-56.

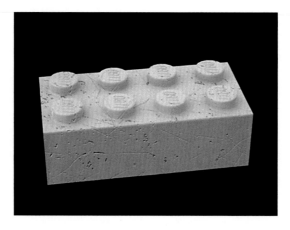

Figure 7-55. *With UV degradation*

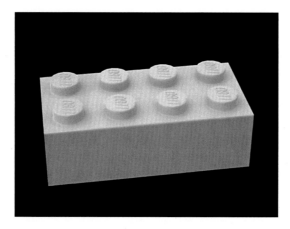

Figure 7-56. *Without UV degradation*

You can control the strength of the UV degradation by typing the minimum (0) and maximum (1) values, as shown in Figure 7-52.

Scratches refer to the marks or abrasions on the surface of LEGO parts.

You can turn ON and OFF the scratches effect, as shown in Figure 7-52. You can compare the scratched LEGO 2*4 brick with the strength of a minimum of 0.5 and a maximum of 1 as shown in Figure 7-57 with the without scratches LEGO 2*4 brick, as shown in Figure 7-58.

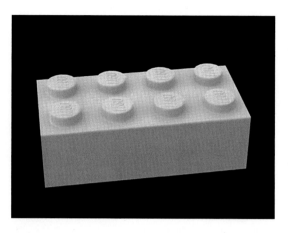

Figure 7-57. *With scratches*

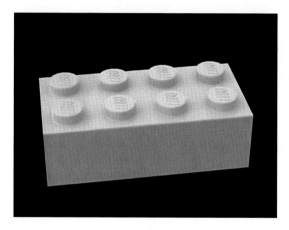

Figure 7-58. *Without scratches*

You can control the strength of scratches by typing the minimum (0) and maximum (1) values, as shown in Figure 7-52.

E. Close the dialog on starting rendering

At the bottom left corner of the render window, there is an option that says "Close this dialog on starting render." If you want to close the render window once you start rendering a model by pressing the render button present at the bottom right corner, then select the check box, as shown in Figure 7-59, or else unselect it.

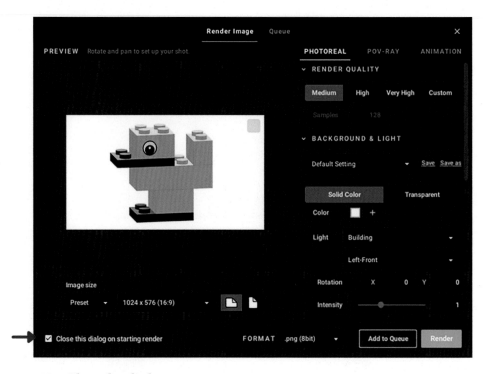

Figure 7-59. *Close the dialog*

F. Format

Before starting rendering, you can also set the format of the image or animation by clicking the Format option, as shown in Figure 7-60. It will open a dropdown menu with different format options.

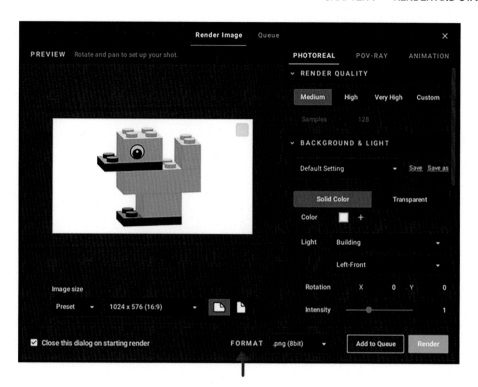

Figure 7-60. *Image or animation format*

For **photoreal,** you will get four format options, that is, .png(8 bit), .png(16 bit), .jpg, and .bmp. For **POV-Ray** you will get three format options, that is, .png(8 bit), .jpg, and .bmp, and for **animation,** you will get five format options, that is, .gif, .mp4, .mov, .png(8 bit) transparent, and .png(16 bit) transparent.

BMP (Bitmap Image File) files contain large, raw, high-quality image, which is uncompressed and lossless. **JPG or JPEG (Joint Photographic Experts Group)** files automatically compress, so they're generally smaller and of lower quality. **PNG (Portable Network Graphics)** is a raster graphic similar to a. JPG image, but is compressed with lossless compression and supports transparency. The main difference between an 8-bit image and a 16-bit image is the number of tones available for a given color. An 8-bit image is made up of fewer tones than a 16-bit image.

I have used the photoreal rendering engine to render an image in four different formats, that is, .bmp, .jpg, .png (8 bit), and .png(16 bit). The dimension of all the images is 800*600. You may not be able to see the clear difference in the image quality in the printed form, but you will be able to see it clearly in the digital form.

After rendering, I got the size of the .bmp image as 1.4 MB and it will be the best among all four formats, as shown in Figure 7-61. The .jpg format image size is 22KB and the quality of the image will be low, as shown in Figure 7-62. The .png (8 bit) and .png(16 bit) look the same, but the image size of the.png(8 bit) is 180 KB and .png(16 bit) is 1.4 MB, as shown in Figures 7-63 and 7-64. The size of the 8-bit and 16-bit image formats itself gives a clear difference.

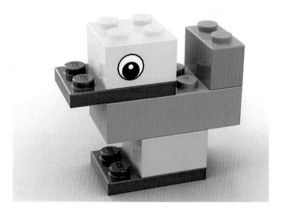

Figure 7-61. *.bmp image format*

Figure 7-62. *.jpg image format*

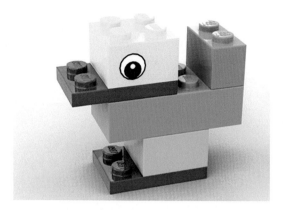

Figure 7-63. *.png (8 bit) image format*

Figure 7-64. *.png (16 bit) image format*

G. Queue

Once you finish setting up all the options in photoreal or POV-Ray or animation, you can click the **add to queue** button which is present at the bottom right corner of the render window, as shown in Figure 7-60. After that, you can click the **queue** option available at the top center, as shown in Figure 7-65. Here you will see all the models which you added to a queue for rendering. To start rendering, you need to click the **green render queue** button, as shown in Figure 7-65.

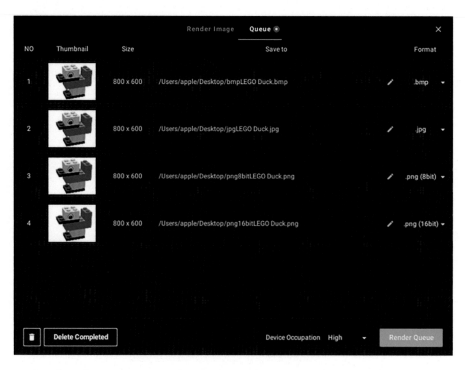

Figure 7-65. *Render queue*

Once it starts rendering, you can see the rendering name on the first file, as shown in Figure 7-66. It renders only one file at a time. You can also see the serial no., thumbnail, size, file location, and format of the file.

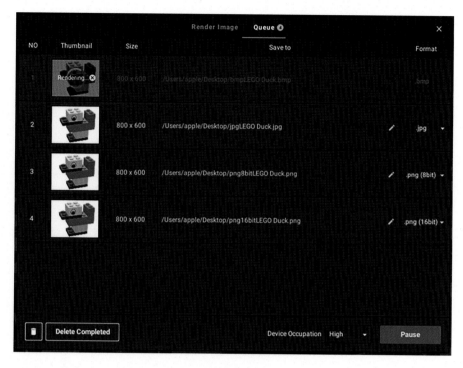

Figure 7-66. *Delete and pause rendering queue*

If you want to delete any file or delete only completed files, then you can use the delete options available in the bottom left corner of the queue window. You can also pause the rendering by pressing the pause button available in the bottom right corner of the queue window, as shown in Figure 7-66.

ADD TO QUEUE AND RENDER BUTTONS

There are two options available in the render window through which you can start rendering. The first one is "**Add to Queue**" and the second is "**Render**," as shown in Figure 7-67. Add to queue will render the files in the background so it will be easy for you to work in the Studio, and the render button will render the file in the foreground.

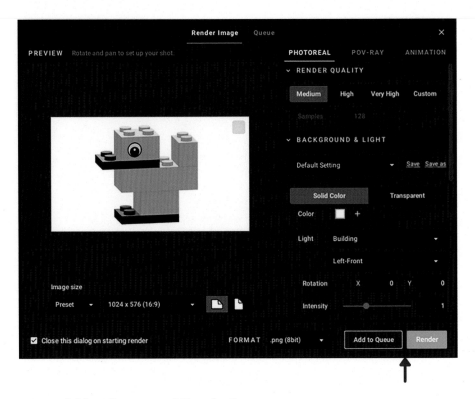

Figure 7-67. *Add to Queue and Render buttons*

Stability Test

When you click the stability option available next to the render option, then a new small window will open in the viewport, as shown in Figure 7-68. Once you click the stability option, the model will convert into translucent.

Figure 7-68. *Stability option*

In the duck model, as shown in Figure 7-68, there is no clutch power issues as all the bricks are connected with each other properly and you can also see zero clutch power issues in stability window, as shown in Figure 7-69.

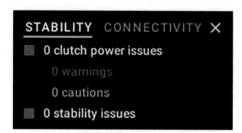

Figure 7-69. *Clutch power and stability issues of duck model*

The green circle under the model, as shown in Figure 7-68, represents the stability of the model. As there are no stability issues, you can see zero stability issues, as shown in Figure 7-69. The darker the color of the green circle, the stronger the stability of the model.

As there are no detached parts in the model, it shows zero detached sections, as shown in Figure 7-70.

Figure 7-70. *Connectivity issues of duck model*

To understand the clutch power issues properly, I have used four 2*4 bricks and made a random model, as shown in Figure 7-71. You can see the first brick is translucent in color as that is stable, the second brick turned red as there is a warning for clutch power issues, and the third and fourth bricks, which are connected on only one stud, turned pink as there are cautions for clutch power issues, as shown in Figure 7-71.

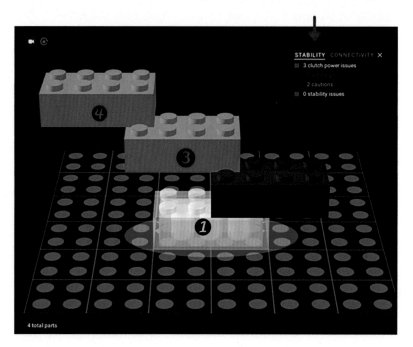

Figure 7-71. *Clutch power issues*

The darker the part color, the weaker the connection point.

To understand the stability issues properly, I have used three 2*4 bricks and made four different models. As shown in Figures 7-72, 7-73, and 7-74, stability issues are zero. But all three models are at different levels of stability. You can also observe the intensity of the green color circle forming under the model is different. The darker the green color circle, the better the stability.

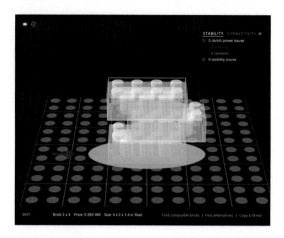

Figure 7-72. *Most stable model*

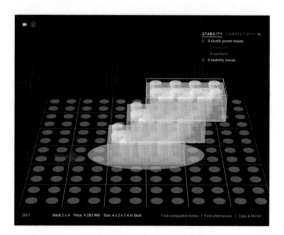

Figure 7-73. *Medium stable model*

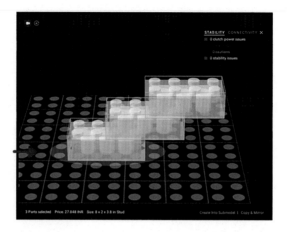

Figure 7-74. *Least stable model*

As shown in Figure 7-75, the green circle changes to red and it shows a stability issue as the model is unstable. The darker the red color circle, the lesser the stability.

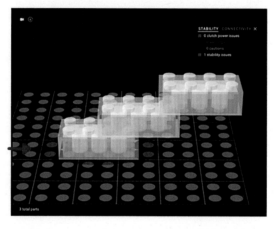

Figure 7-75. *Unstable model*

If any part is not connected with the main model, then the Studio will show the connectivity issue as a detached section. If there are multiple models in the viewport, the model with the greater number of parts will be considered as the main model. The detached section will be highlighted with pink color, as shown in Figure 7-76.

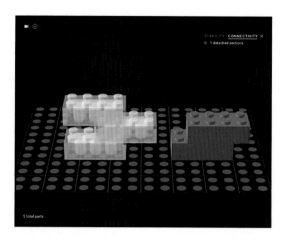

Figure 7-76. *Connectivity issues*

Sometimes Studio shows a few stability issues which may or may not be present in the physical model.

Conclusion

In this chapter, you learned about different rendering engines and also how to animate your model. Checking the stability of the model using a stability tool is one of the most important tasks before finalizing the model.

In the next chapter, you will learn about instruction maker and mosaic.

CHAPTER 8

Instruction and Mosaic

In this chapter, I will explain instruction and mosaic tools in detail which are situated at the top of the Studio user interface, as shown in Figure 8-1.

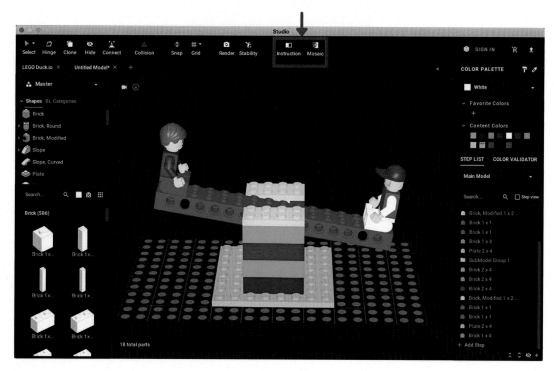

Figure 8-1. *Instruction and mosaic tools*

Instruction

There are two ways through which you can create instruction for your model. The first way is you can create the steps for your model in the step list (Chapter 6) while building a model, as shown in Figure 8-2, and directly move to page design to create the pdf file of your instructions.

© Vishnu Agarwal 2023
V. Agarwal, *The Art of Virtual LEGO Design*, https://doi.org/10.1007/978-1-4842-8777-4_8

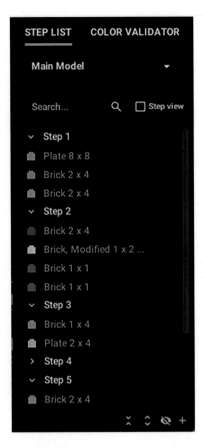

Figure 8-2. *Creating steps in step list*

Another way to create instructions is using the step editor and then using page design to create the pdf file of your instructions. In this case, no need to create steps while building the model. You can build the whole model in a single step, as shown in Figure 8-3, and later use the step editor.

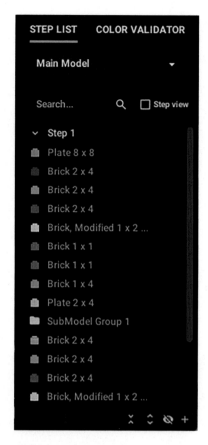

Figure 8-3. *Building a model in single step*

Sometimes it is difficult to analyze which part will go to which step. In that case, it's a good idea to focus on building the model and later create the steps and instructions. If you have already created the steps in the step list and later want to modify them then it can also be done in the step editor.

When you click the instruction icon, as shown in Figure 8-1, a new window will open, as shown in Figure 8-4. It is the caution window that says "The current building mode will be switched to instruction maker mode. Do you want to proceed?" If you want to proceed to the instruction maker mode, then click OK, proceed, or else click cancel.

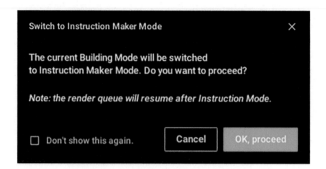

Figure 8-4. *Switch to instruction maker mode caution window*

This caution window will appear when you switch to instruction maker mode for the first time. If you don't want it to appear again, then select the check box which says "Don't show this again," as shown in Figure 8-4.

When you enter the instruction maker, you will get two sections, step editor, as shown in Figure 8-5, and page design, as shown in Figure 8-6.

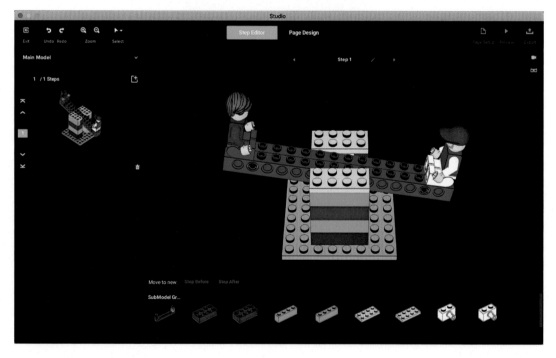

Figure 8-5. *Step editor*

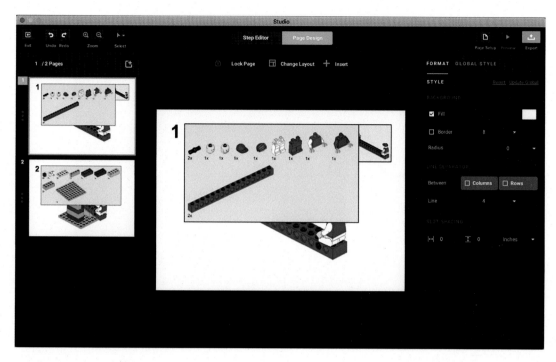

Figure 8-6. *Page design*

A. Step Editor

The step editor is used to create steps for your model. Once your model is ready, you can assign steps to each part of the model. I have mentioned the names of important parts of the step editor, as shown in Figure 8-7.

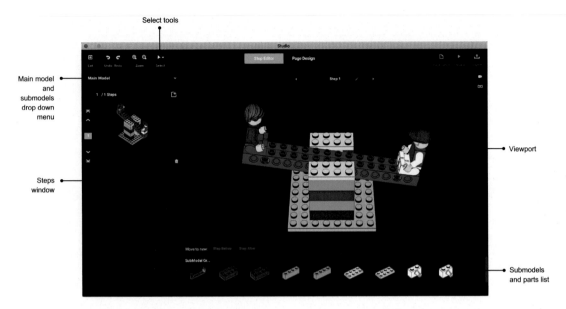

Figure 8-7. *Step editor user interface*

- **Creating Steps**

To create steps for your model, you need to plan if you want to start creating steps from the first step to the last step or from the last step to the first step.

I have selected to go from the first step to the last step to create the steps for the seesaw model. The first part I have selected to create the first step is an 8*8 baseplate highlighted with a blue outline, as shown in Figure 8-8. After that, you can click "move to new: **step before**."

Figure 8-8. *Selecting first part to create step*

You can select the parts of the model directly in the viewport or you can also select the parts in the parts list present at the bottom of the step editor.

After clicking on "move to new: step before," the 8*8 baseplate will be added to the first step, as shown in the steps window, and it will change to translucent color in step 2, as shown in Figure 8-9.

Figure 8-9. *8*8 baseplate changed to translucent*

Similarly, when I selected 2*4 purple brick and clicked on "move to new: step before," the 2*4 purple brick was added to the second step, as shown in the steps window, and it was changed to translucent color in step 3, as shown in Figure 8-10.

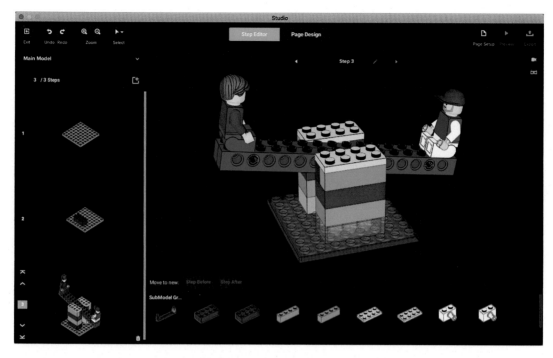

Figure 8-10. *2*4 purple brick changed to translucent*

In the same way, you can select each part of your model to create the steps. Translucent parts represent that you have already used those parts to create a step. Another way to see the translucent part is that the colored part in the current step is the new part added to your model in that step and the translucent parts are the parts of the previous steps.

If you want to create the steps from the last step to the first step then you need to use the "Move to new: Step After" option to create the steps of your model.

- **Create a Submodel and Divide into Steps**

When you select two or more parts in a model, the "create a submodel" and "divide into steps" options will appear in the right corner above the parts list, as shown in Figure 8-11.

Figure 8-11. *Create a submodel and divide into steps options*

Using the "create a submodel" option, you can select parts to create a submodel. You learned about how to create a submodel in Chapter 5 also.

When you select the multiple parts or the whole model and then click the "Divide into steps" option, the Studio will create the steps automatically for you, as shown in Figure 8-11.

But one disadvantage of "Divide into steps" is that sometimes automatically generated steps are not in the correct sequence. It works best with small models, but it may not work properly with big models.

- **Models Drop-down Menu**

"Models drop-down menu" is situated at the upper left corner of the step editor user interface, as shown in Figure 8-12. When you click this drop-down menu, you will get the names of all the submodels along with the main model.

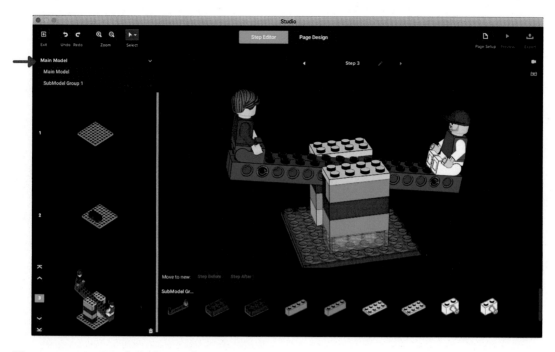

Figure 8-12. *Models drop-down menu*

- **Creating Steps for Submodels**

To create the steps for a submodel, you need to open the submodel section by selecting the name of the submodel from the models drop-down menu, as shown in Figure 8-12. You can also open the submodel section by selecting the submodel in the step editor parts list and then clicking on view steps, as shown in Figure 8-13.

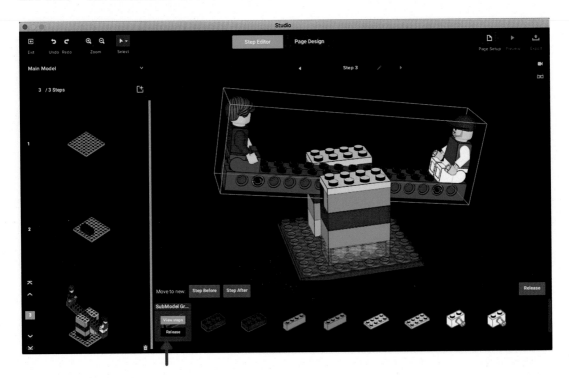

Figure 8-13. *View steps for submodel*

After opening the submodel section, you can select each part of the submodel to create the steps or you can also use the "divide into steps" option to create steps as explained earlier and shown in Figure 8-14.

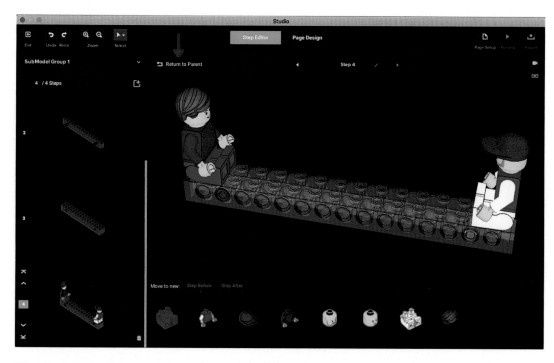

Figure 8-14. *Creating steps for submodel and return to parent*

After creating the steps of the submodel, you can return to the main model by clicking the "return to parent" option, as shown in Figure 8-14.

- **New Parts Highlight and Viewport Control**

When new parts will be added to the current step, the parts will be highlighted with their standard color and the previous steps' parts will turn translucent color, as shown in Figure 8-15.

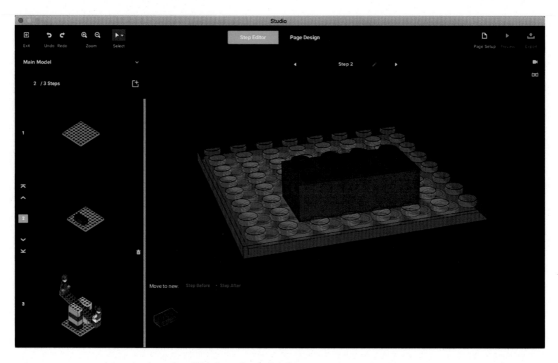

Figure 8-15. *New parts highlighted with their standard color*

Another way the Studio will highlight the new parts is with a red color outline, and the previous steps' parts will not turn translucent color, as shown in Figure 8-16.

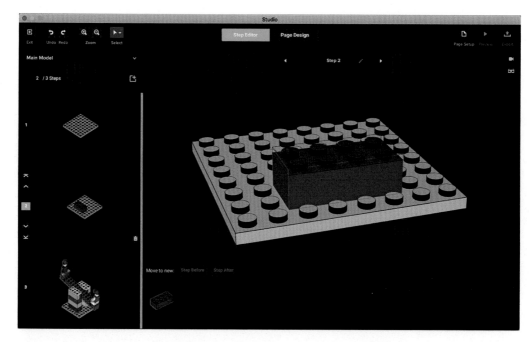

Figure 8-16. *New parts highlighted with the red color outline*

You can switch between the two types of "new parts highlight" using the goggles button, as shown in Figure 8-17.

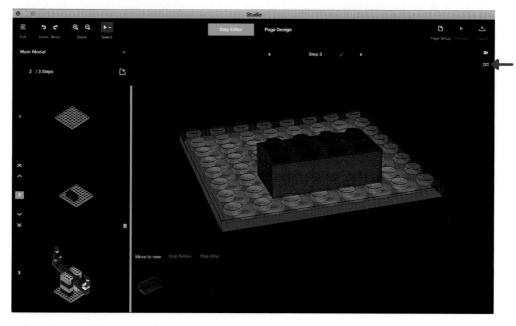

Figure 8-17. *New parts highlight button*

To change the orientation of the view of the model, you need to click the viewport controls button, as shown in Figure 8-18. You can switch the orientation to Free View, Front View, Back View, Left View, Right View, Bottom View, Top View, and Orthogonal View.

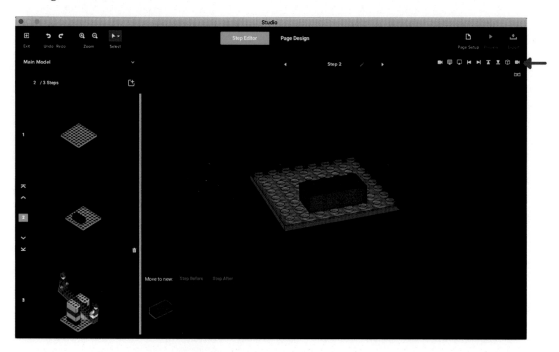

Figure 8-18.   *Viewport controls*

- **Move a Part to a Different Step**

There are three different ways you can move a part from one step to another. You can move single or multiple parts at the same time to a different step.

The first way to move a part to a different step is by right-clicking on the part in the viewport and selecting the option based on your requirements to move a part to a different step.

I have selected a 2*4 Azure color brick in the seesaw model and right-clicked on it, as shown in Figure 8-19. After that, you will get different options to move that part. You can move the part to a new step before, a new step after, step before, step after, first step, last step or you can move the part to any specific step, as shown in Figure 8-19.

Figure 8-19. *Right click on the part to move a part*

The second way to move a part to a different step is by dragging the part from the viewport to the specific step in the steps window.

I have selected a 2*4 Azure color brick in the seesaw model, left-clicked on it, and started dragging it. As soon as I started dragging, the mouse cursor changed to a palm holding a 1*1 brick, as shown in Figure 8-20. After that, I dragged the 2*4 Azure brick to step 2 in the steps window and released the left click, as shown in Figure 8-21.

Figure 8-20. *Drag the part from the viewport to move a part*

Figure 8-21. *Drop the part to different step in the steps window*

The third way to move a part to a different step is by dragging the part from the parts and submodel list to the specific step in the steps window.

I have selected a 2*4 Azure color brick in the parts and submodel list, left-clicked on it, and started dragging it. As soon as I started dragging the mouse cursor changed to the cursor holding a 1*1 brick, as shown in Figure 8-22. After that, I dragged the 2*4 Azure brick to step 2 in the steps window and released the left click, as shown in Figure 8-23.

Figure 8-22. *Drag the part from the parts and submodel list to move a part*

Figure 8-23. *Drop the part to different step in the steps window*

After moving the 2*4 Azure color brick to step 2 using any one of the ways explained earlier, the 2*4 Azure color brick will be the part of step 2, and in step 3, it will turn translucent color, as shown in Figure 8-24.

Figure 8-24. *2*4 Azure color brick turns translucent*

- **Changing the Step Number**

The first way to change the step number of any step is first you need to select the step which you want to change in the steps window. Then use the arrow buttons to shift the current step to the first step, swap with the previous step, swap with the next step, or shift the current step to the last step, as shown in Figure 8-25.

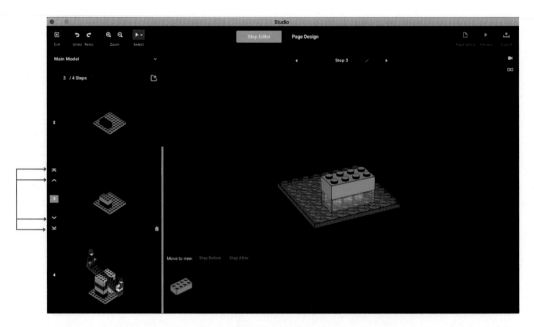

Figure 8-25. *Changing the step number using arrow buttons*

Another way to change the step number of any step is by clicking on the step number in the steps window and typing the new step number, as shown in Figure 8-26.

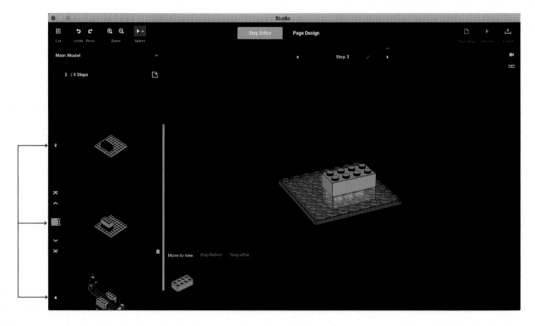

Figure 8-26. *Changing the step number by typing the new step number*

- **Delete and Add a Step**

To delete any step, you need to select that step in the steps window and then click the delete icon, as shown in Figure 8-27.

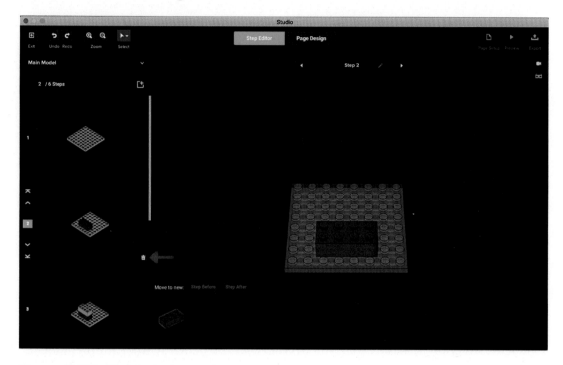

Figure 8-27. *Delete a step*

To add a new step, you need to click the "+" button situated above the steps window. Once you click this button, a new empty step will be created next to the selected step in the steps window, as shown in Figure 8-28.

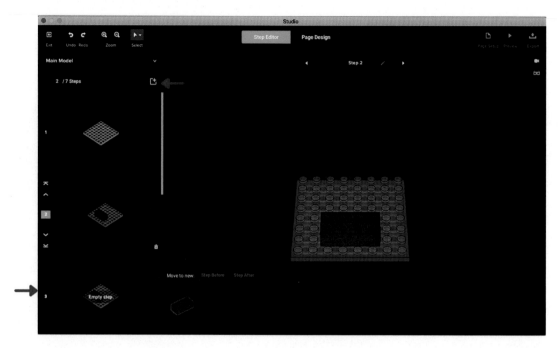

Figure 8-28. *Add a step*

- **Step Description and Changing the Steps in Viewport**

To add the description for any step, you need to click the pencil symbol button in the viewport, as shown in Figure 8-29. Once you click that pencil symbol, a new window will appear where you can write the step description, as shown in Figure 8-29.

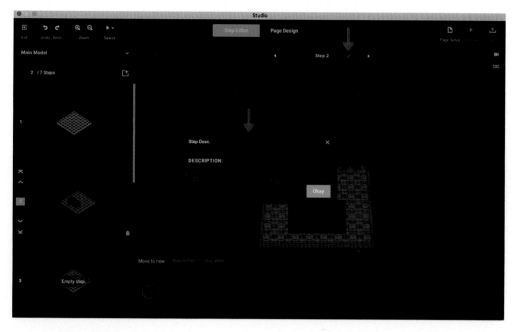

Figure 8-29. *Step description*

To change the steps in the viewport, you can click the left and right arrow buttons, as shown in Figure 8-30.

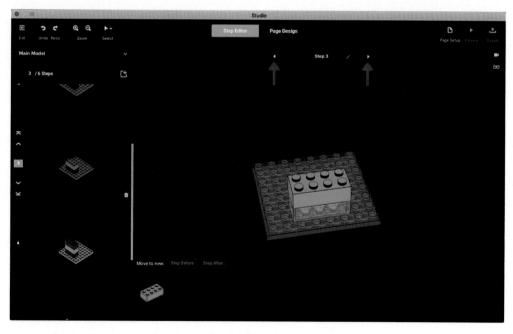

Figure 8-30. *Changing the steps in the viewport*

- **Select Tools**

Select tools plays a very important role in creating steps. You can open the select tools by clicking the select option situated at the top left of the step editor user interface, as shown in Figure 8-31. I have already explained in detail about select tools in Chapter 2. You can refer to Chapter 2 for more details about select tools.

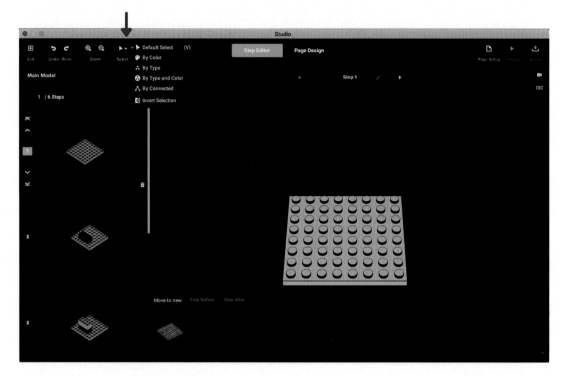

Figure 8-31. *Select tools*

- **Undo, Redo, Zoom In, and Zoom Out**

You can undo and redo any action by clicking the undo and redo buttons situated at the top left of the step editor user interface, as shown in Figure 8-32. Undo function is used to reverse any action and the redo function is used to restore any action.

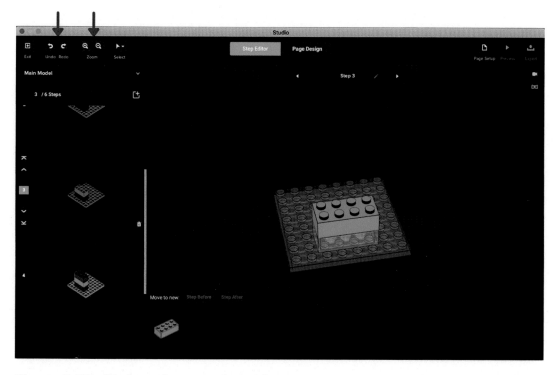

Figure 8-32. *Undo, redo, zoom in, and zoom out*

Using zoom in and zoom out buttons you can increase and decrease the models' size in the viewport. Zoom in and zoom out buttons are next to the undo and redo buttons, as shown in Figure 8-32.

- **Exit**

Exit button is situated at the top-left corner of the step editor user interface, as shown in Figure 8-33. When you click the "exit" button, the current step editor mode will switch to building mode.

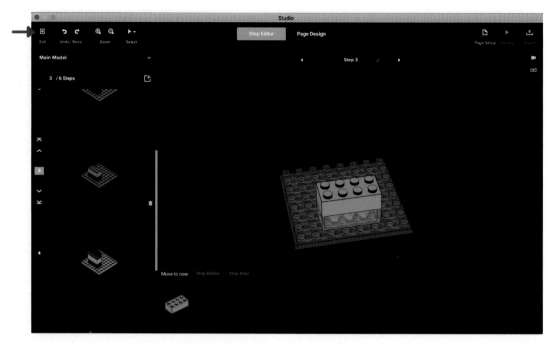

Figure 8-33. *Exit from step editor*

B. Page Design

The page design is used to make your instructions look attractive and clear. You can also create pdf instructions for your model. Once you finish creating steps for your model in the **step editor**, you can click **page design** to edit the instruction pages, as shown in Figure 8-34.

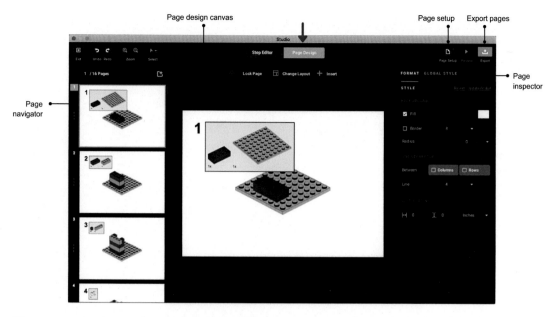

Figure 8-34. *Page design user interface*

- **Add and Delete a Page**

There are multiple ways you can add and delete a page. The first way to add a page is by clicking the "+" **button** situated at the top of the page navigator, as shown in Figure 8-35.

When you click this "+" button, a new page will be added after the selected page, as shown in Figure 8-35.

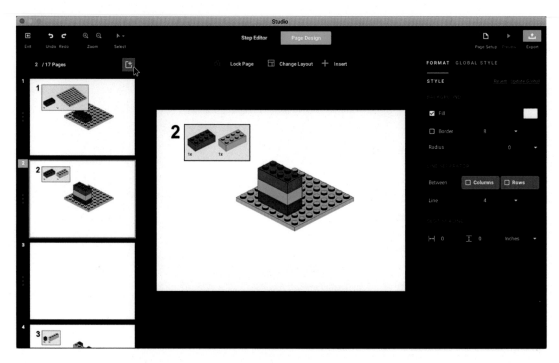

Figure 8-35. *Add a page using "+" button*

The second way to add and delete a page is by right-clicking the page in the page navigator, as shown in Figure 8-36. In this case, a new page will be added before the selected page.

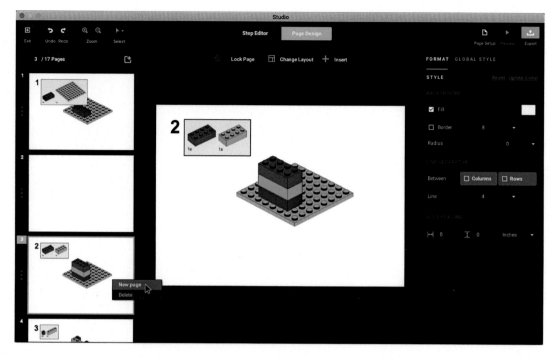

Figure 8-36. *Add and delete a page using right click on the page*

You cannot delete a page with steps as shown in Figure 8-36.

The third way to add and delete a page is by clicking on the three dots situated on the left side of the page in the page navigator, as shown in Figure 8-37. A new page can be added before or after the selected page by selecting the option insert page before or after.

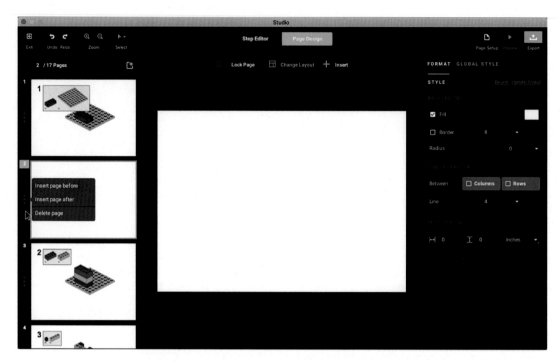

Figure 8-37. *Add and delete a page by clicking on three dots*

You can only delete a page with no steps, as shown in Figure 8-37.

- **Lock and Unlock the Page**

When you click on the **lock page** option, as shown in Figure 8-38, you won't be able to edit the selected page.

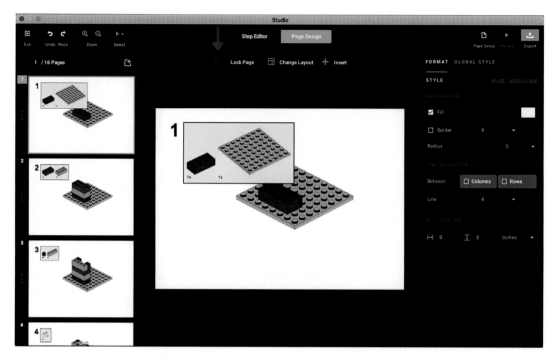

Figure 8-38. *Lock page option*

After clicking the "lock page" option, the selected page will be locked and the lock symbol will appear in the pages list, as shown in Figure 8-39. You will not be able to **format** the locked page, but the changes applied in the **global style** will be applied to the locked page also.

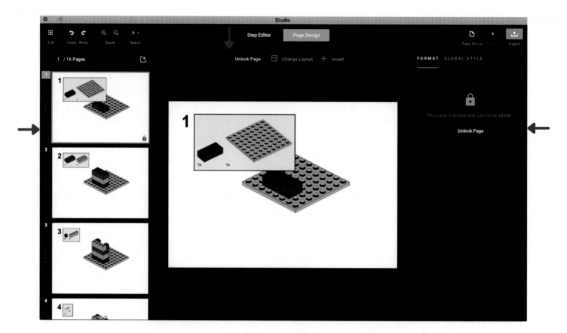

Figure 8-39. *Unlock page option*

To unlock the page, you need to click on the ***unlock page*** option, as shown in Figure 8-39.

- **Change Layout**

To change the page layout, you need to click the **change layout** option situated next to the **lock page** option, as shown in Figure 8-40. After that, a new window will open which will give you different layout options to choose from. You can select one to six steps for a page layout available in different combinations, as shown in Figure 8-40.

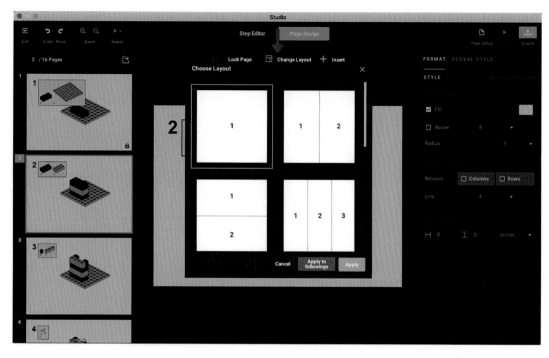

Figure 8-40. *Changing page layout*

After selecting the page layout if you click the **apply** button, then the layout will change only for the selected page, and if you click **apply for followings**, then the layout will change for the current and all the pages following the current page.

- **Insert**

The **insert** option is situated at the top center of the page design user interface. When you click the insert option, you will get seven options to insert into your page design, as shown in Figure 8-41. Let's understand each one of them one by one.

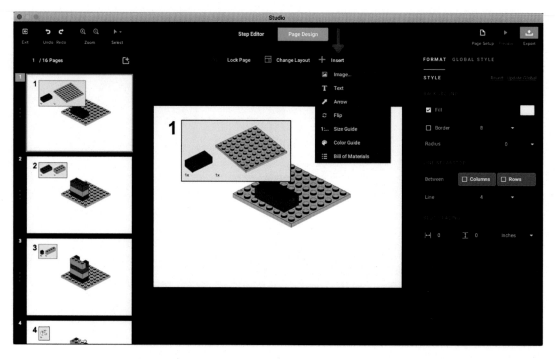

Figure 8-41. *Insert options*

a. **Insert an Image**

You can add an image to any page using the **insert image** option, as shown in Figure 8-41. I have added a page before the first step and used the insert image option to add an image, as shown in Figure 8-42. The image is the rendered image of the seesaw model.

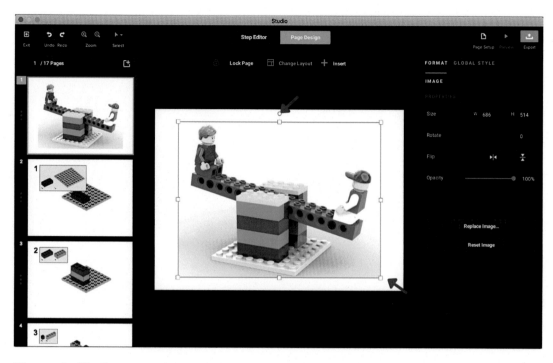

Figure 8-42. *Insert an image*

After adding an image to the page, when you click on the image, you will get image properties options under the format section, as shown in Figure 8-42. You can change the size, rotate, flip, and change the opacity level of the image. You can also replace the image and reset the properties of the image.

You can also change the size of the image by stretching the corners of the image and rotate the image by rotating the small circle at the top of the image in the page canvas, as shown in Figure 8-42.

To cut, copy, or delete the image, you need to right-click on the image and select the correct option, as shown in Figure 8-43. After cutting or copying the image, if you want to paste it on a different or same page, then right-click on that page and select the paste option.

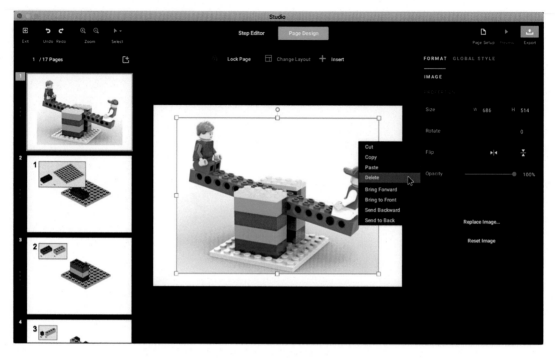

Figure 8-43. *Cut, copy, paste, and delete the image*

b. **Insert Text**

You can add text to any page using the ***insert text*** option, as shown in Figure 8-41. After clicking the insert text option, you will get a text box and you can type whatever you want, as shown in Figure 8-44. You can left-click and hold on to the text box to drag it. You can also change the size of the text box by stretching the corners and rotate by rotating the small circle at the top of the text box.

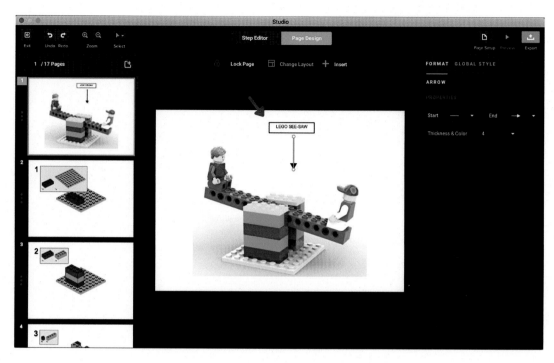

Figure 8-44. *Insert text*

When you click on the text box, you will also get the edit options under the format section, as shown in Figure 8-44. You can modify the text box, text font, and text alignment.

To cut, copy, or delete the text box, you need to right-click it and select the correct option. After cutting or copying the text box, if you want to paste it on a different or same page, right-click on that page and select the paste option.

c. **Insert Arrow**

You can add an arrow using the **insert arrow** option, as shown in Figure 8-41. After clicking on the insert arrow option, a black arrow will appear on the page, as shown in Figure 8-45. You can left-click and hold on to the arrow to drag it. You can also change the size and direction of the arrow by stretching the small circle at the top and bottom of the arrow.

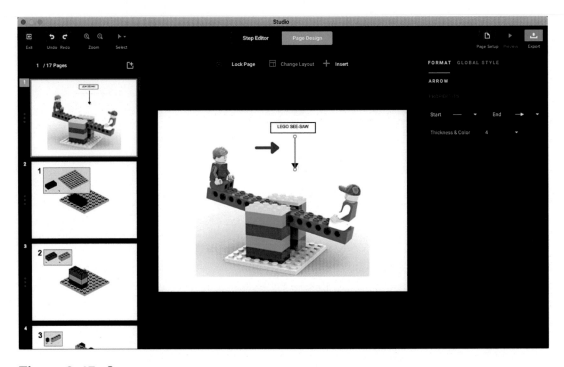

Figure 8-45. *Insert arrow*

When you click the arrow, you will also get the edit options under the format section, as shown in Figure 8-45. You can modify the start and end arrow style and also the arrow thickness and color.

To cut, copy, or delete the arrow, you need to right-click the arrow and select the correct option. After cutting or copying the arrow, if you want to paste it on a different or same page, then right-click on that page and select the paste option.

d. **Insert Flip**

You can add a flip image to any page using the **insert flip** option, as shown in Figure 8-41.

After adding a flip image to the page, when you click on the flip image, you will get properties options under the format section, as shown in Figure 8-46. You can change the size, rotate, flip, and change the opacity level of the flip image. You can also replace the image and reset the properties of the image.

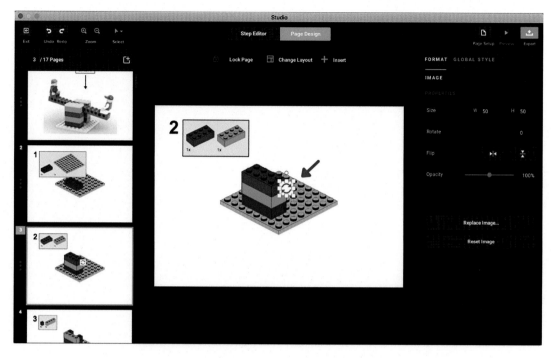

Figure 8-46. *Insert flip icon*

You can left-click and hold on to the flip image to drag it to different locations on the page. You can also change the size of the flip image by stretching the corners of the image and rotate it by rotating the small circle at the top of the image in the page canvas, as shown in Figure 8-46.

To cut, copy, or delete the flip image, you need to right-click the flip image and select the correct option. After cutting or copying the flip image, if you want to paste it on a different or the same page, right-click on that page and select the paste option.

e. **Insert 1:1 Size Guide**

You can add a 1:1 size guide to any page using the **insert 1:1 size guide** option, as shown in Figure 8-41. It is a good idea to add the size guide for any part to the page if you think there will be any confusion while building the model. I have used a size 5 axle in the seesaw model, but it's difficult to understand the axle size by seeing the parts list, as shown in Figure 8-47. After setting up the page size, you can print the instruction to get the correct 1:1 size guide.

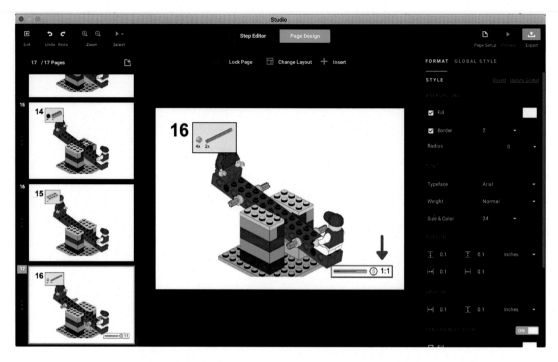

Figure 8-47. *Insert 1:1 size guidey*

After adding a size guide to the page, when you click on the size guide, you will get edit options under the format section, as shown in Figure 8-47. You can change the background, font, padding, spacing, and length indicator of the selected size guide box. You will also get the size guide edit options under the global style section, and if you make any changes under the global style section, the changes will apply to all the size guides.

You can left-click and hold on to the size guide box to drag it to different locations on the page. To cut, copy, or delete the size guide, you need to right-click it and select the correct option. After cutting or copying the size guide, if you want to paste it on a different or the same page, then right-click on that page and select the paste option.

f. **Insert Color Guide**

You can add the color guide to any page using the ***insert-color guide*** option, as shown in Figure 8-41. After clicking the insert-color guide option, a new window will open which will give you the list of all the parts added in that step with their color names, as shown in Figure 8-48. You can select the check box of the parts for which you want to add the color guide on the page.

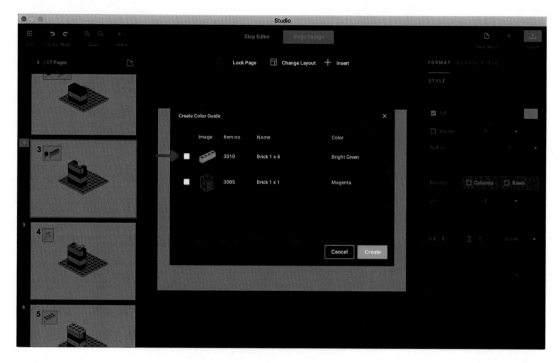

Figure 8-48. *Insert color guide window*

After selecting the parts' check box, click the create option, as shown in Figure 8-48. After clicking the create option, you will get the color guide box on the page, as shown in Figure 8-49.

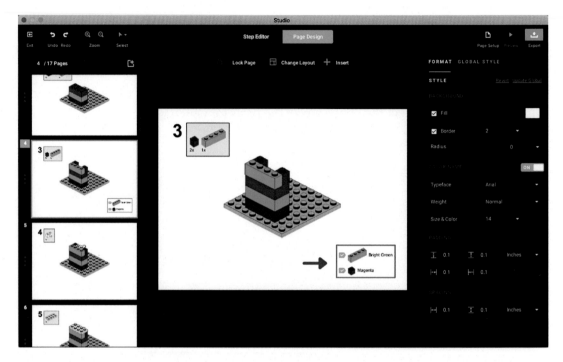

Figure 8-49. *Color guide box*

After adding the color guide to the page, when you click on the color guide, you will get edit options under the format section, as shown in Figure 8-49. You can edit the background, color name, padding, and spacing of the selected color guide box. You will also get the color guide edit options under the global style section and if you do any changes under the global style section, the changes will apply to all the color guides.

You can left-click and hold on to the color guide box to drag it to different locations on the page. To cut, copy, or delete the color guide box, you need to right-click on it and select the correct option. After cutting or copying the color guide box if you want to paste it on a different or the same page, then right-click on that page and select the paste option.

g. **Insert Bill of Materials**

You can add the bill of materials using the **insert – bill of materials** option, as shown in Figure 8-41. I have added a page after the last step and used the insert – bill of materials option. The bill of materials will give you a list of all the parts used in the model, as shown in Figure 8-50.

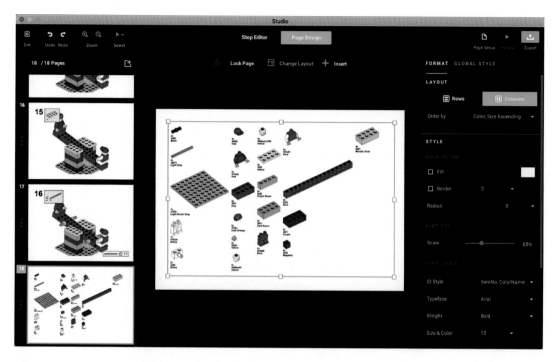

Figure 8-50. *Insert bill of materials*

After adding the bill of materials to the page when you click on it, you will get edit options under the format section, as shown in Figure 8-50. You can change the layout, background, part size, part count, padding, and spacing of the bill of materials.

You can change the size of the bill of materials box without affecting the size of the parts by stretching the corners of the bill of materials box, as shown in Figure 8-50.

To delete the bill of materials, you need to right-click on it and select the delete option. You cannot cut, copy, and paste the bill of materials.

BRING FORWARD AND SEND BACKWARD

You can use the bring forward, bring to front, send backward, and send to back options to arrange the images or any other elements, that is, step list, step number, submodel preview, etc., forward or backward to each other, based on your requirements.

I have selected a page where the model image is behind the parts list, as shown in Figure 8-51.

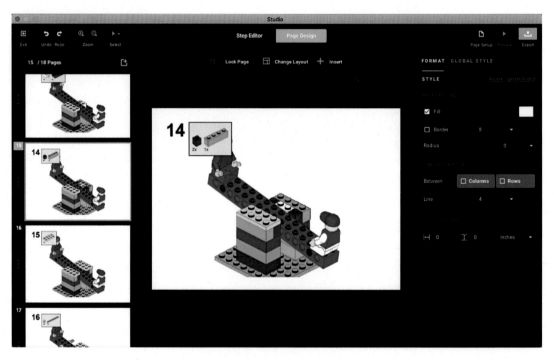

Figure 8-51. *Model image behind the parts list*

Now, right-click the parts list and select the **send back** option, as shown in Figure 8-52.

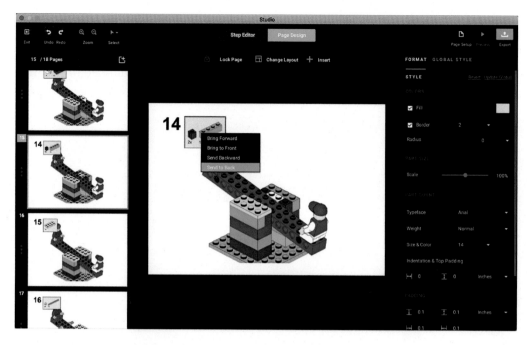

Figure 8-52. *Sending parts list behind the model image*

After that, the parts list will go behind the model image, as shown in Figure 8-53.

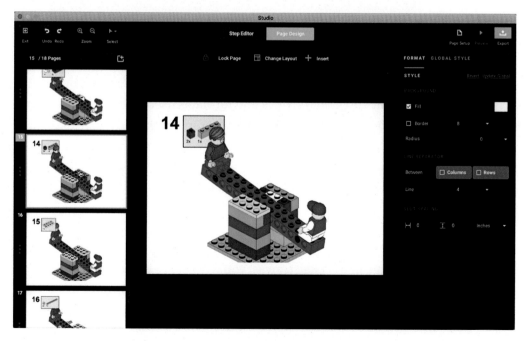

Figure 8-53. *Parts list behind the model image*

- **Page Inspector**

The page inspector is situated at the right side of the page design user interface, as shown in Figure 8-54. To edit all the elements in the page design, you need to use the page inspector options.

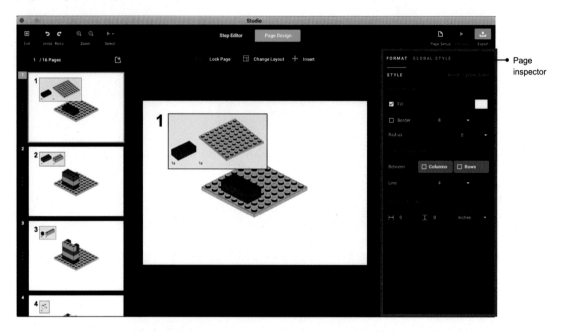

Figure 8-54. *Page inspector*

In the page inspector, there are two sections: ***format*** and ***global style.*** The main difference between format and global style is that format is used only to change or modify the elements of the selected page, whereas changes in the global style will apply to all the pages.

If you make any changes to the elements of the page using the format option, the changes done in the global style will not apply to the page that you edited using the format option.

a. **Page**

When you click on the page in the page canvas, you will get the edit options under the format section, as shown in Figure 8-55. You can change the **background** by selecting the background color, adding the border, and changing the radius of the border.

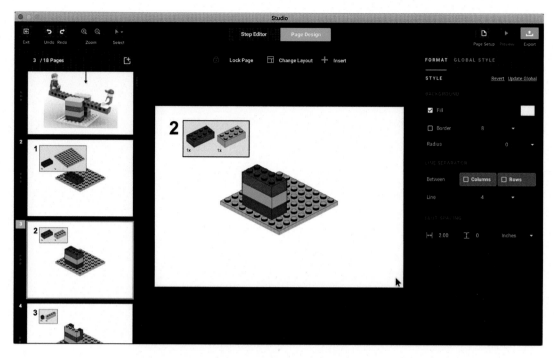

Figure 8-55. *Changing page style using the format option*

Using a **line separator**, you can add a line between columns and rows of the steps when you change the page layout to two or more steps on a page, as shown in Figure 8-56. Also, using the **slot spacing** option, you can increase or decrease the space between the steps.

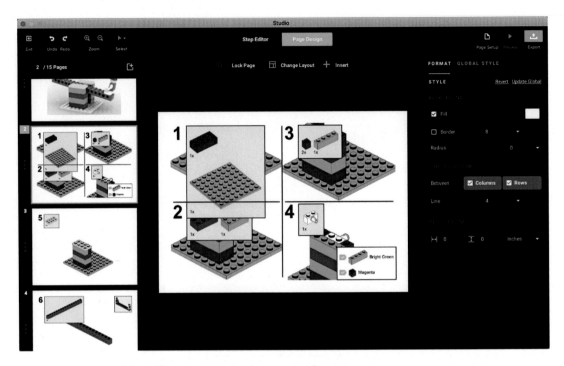

Figure 8-56. *Adding line separator between the steps*

You can also edit the page style under the global style section, as shown in Figure 8-57. You will get all the edit options that you got under the format section. But the changes done under the global style section will apply to all other pages.

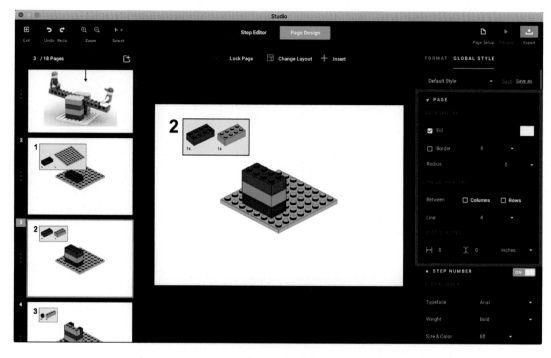

Figure 8-57. *Changing page style using global style option*

b. **Revert and Update Global**

Revert and update global options are situated at the top of the format section, as shown in Figure 8-58. Now both the options are in light grey color and inactive because we have not done any changes in the current page.

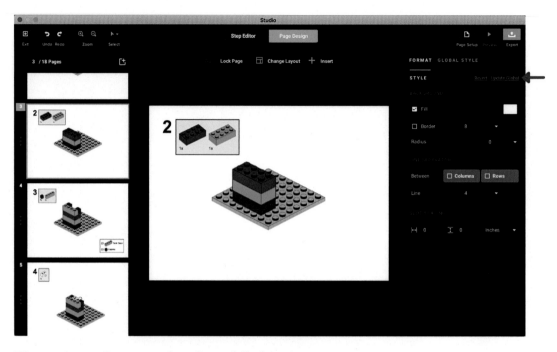

Figure 8-58. *Revert and update global options*

If you want to undo the change, you can click the revert option, and if you want to apply the changes done to the current to all the pages, click the update global option.

I have changed the background of the selected page to purple, as shown in Figure 8-59. Now both revert and update global options turned white and can be used as required. If you click the revert option, the page color will change back to white, as shown in Figure 8-58.

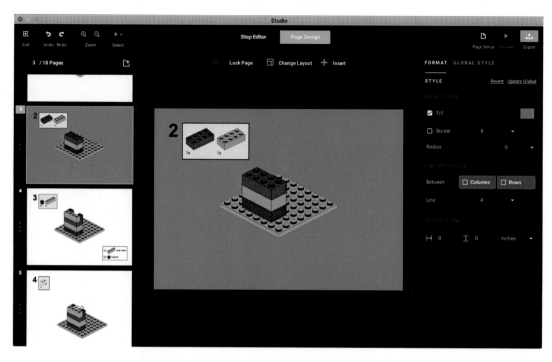

Figure 8-59. *Changing the background color of step 2*

If you click the update global option, all the pages' color will update to purple, as shown in Figure 8-60.

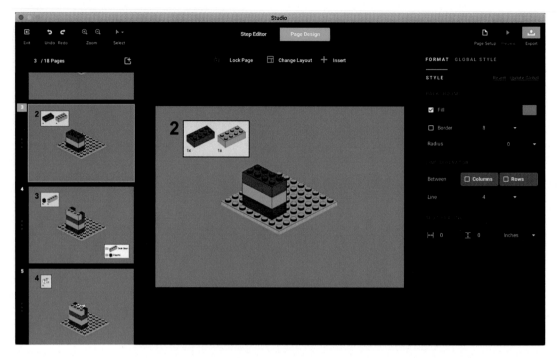

Figure 8-60. *Updating the background colors using update global*

c. **Global Styles Drop-down Menu**

The global styles drop-down menu is situated at the top of the global style section, as shown in Figure 8-61. When you make any changes in the global style section, you can click the save option to save it as the default style.

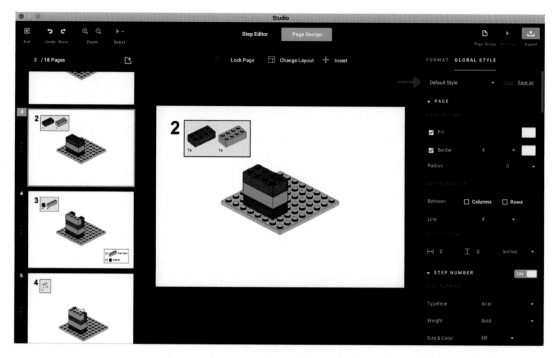

Figure 8-61. *Global styles drop-down menu*

To create a **new custom global style**, first you need to make the required changes under the global style section. I have updated the page border to red color and then clicked the "save as" option present next to the default style drop-down menu. After that, a new window will open where you can type the name of your new custom style, as shown in Figure 8-62. I typed the name as "New style" and then clicked okay.

Figure 8-62. *Creating new custom global style*

After creating a new style, you can see all the new styles under the dropdown menu, as shown in Figure 8-63. If you want to delete any new style which you create, then first you need to select the default style and then you can see a delete icon next to the new styles to delete that style in the drop-down menu.

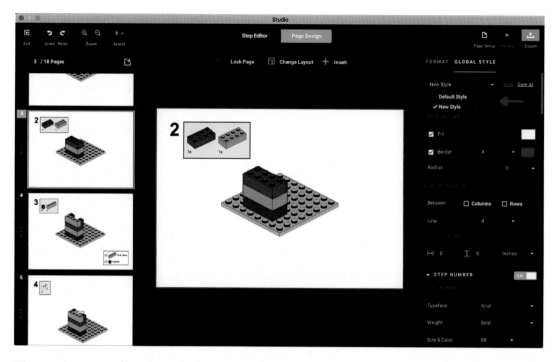

Figure 8-63. *Different styles under global styles drop-down menu*

d. Change Step View

When you click on the step view section of the page, you will get the step view edit options under the format section, as shown in Figure 8-64. To activate the edit options of the step view under the format section you need to click the ***change step view*** button, as shown in Figure 8-64. Under the change step view edit options, you will also get options to turn ON and OFF step number and parts list for the individual pages.

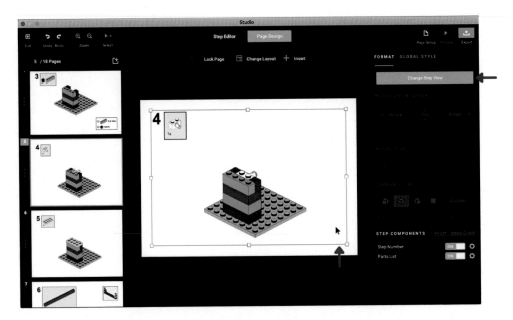

Figure 8-64. *Change step view button*

After clicking the change step view button, you will get all the edit options for step view, as shown in Figure 8-65. You can change the model orientation, model size, and camera setup.

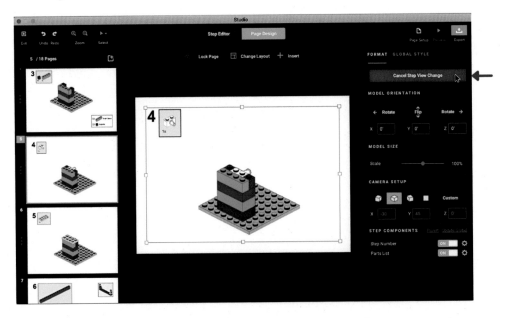

Figure 8-65. *Step view edit options and cancel step view changes*

After changing the step view of the model if you want to revert the changes, you need to click the **cancel step view changes (red button)**, as shown in Figure 8-65.

When you make any changes in the step view, the changes will apply only to the selected and the following steps.

As shown in Figure 8-66, I have changed the model orientation of step 4 and the changes did not apply to the previous steps. The step view changes applied only to the current and following steps.

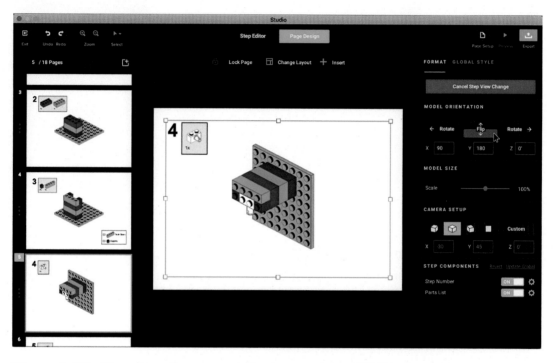

Figure 8-66. *Step view changes applies to current and following steps*

e. Step Number

When you click on the step number of the page, you will get the step number edit options under the format section, as shown in Figure 8-67. You can edit the typeface, weight, and size and color of the step number.

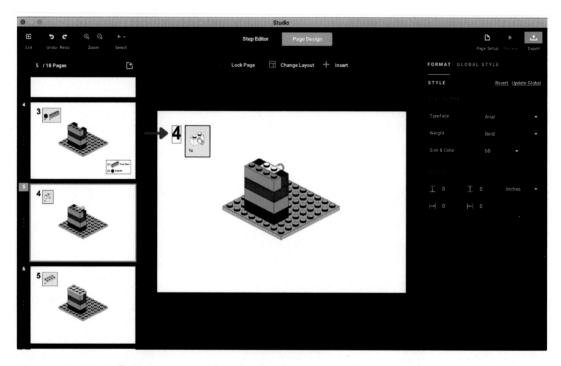

Figure 8-67. *Editing step number under format section*

By default, the step number will be situated in the top-left corner of the page. But if you want to change its position, you can drag it to different corners and use the padding option to modify its distance from the corners.

You can also edit the step number under the global style section, as shown in Figure 8-68. You will get all the edit options that you got under the format section. But the changes done under the global style section will apply to all other pages.

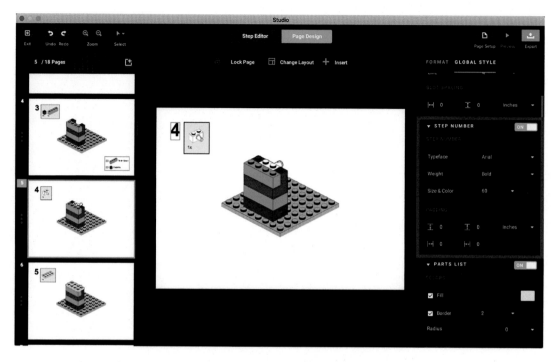

Figure 8-68. *Editing step number under global style section*

If you turn ON or OFF the step number, it will apply to all the pages. But if you want to turn ON or OFF the step number of any specific page then you can do it under the step view format section.

f. **Parts List**

When you click on the parts list of a step on the page, you will get the parts list edit options under the format section, as shown in Figure 8-69. You can edit the background color, part size, and part count of the parts list.

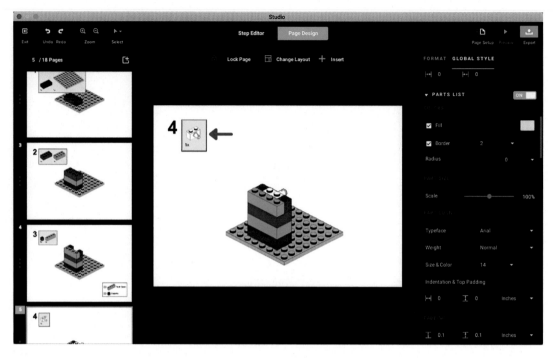

Figure 8-69. *Editing parts list under format section*

By default, the parts list will be situated in the top-left corner of the page, as shown in Figure 8-69. But if you want to change its position, you can drag it to different corners and use the padding option to modify its distance from its box borders. You can also change the padding values of the part number to change the position of the parts list.

You can also edit the parts list under the global style section, as shown in Figure 8-70. You will get all the edit options that you got under the format section. But the changes done under the global style section will apply to all other pages.

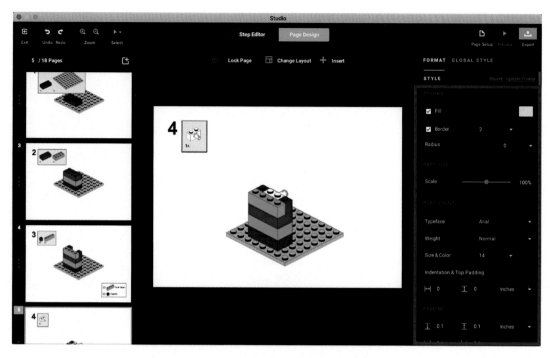

Figure 8-70. *Editing parts list under global style section*

If you turn ON or OFF the parts list, it will apply to all the pages. But if you want to turn ON or OFF the parts list of any specific page, you can do it under the step view format section.

g. **New Part Highlight**

The new part highlight is a feature in the Studio which highlights the new part(s) added in the step. You can choose to turn ON and OFF this feature. You can edit the new parts highlight feature only under the global style section, as shown in Figure 8-71. You can change the thickness and color of the highlighted border.

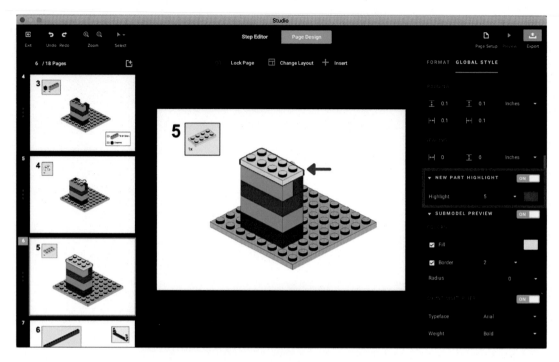

Figure 8-71. *Turn ON the new part highlight*

When the new part highlight feature is ON, the new 2*4 yellow plate in step 5 is highlighted with red color, as shown in Figure 8-71, and when it's OFF, the new 2*4 yellow plate is not highlighted with any color, as shown in Figure 8-72.

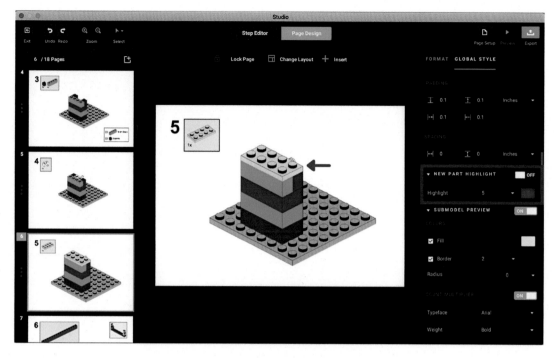

Figure 8-72. *Turn OFF the new part highlight*

h. **Submodel Preview**

When you click the submodel preview box on the page, you will get the edit options under the format section, as shown in Figure 8-73. You can change the model orientation, model size, and camera setup.

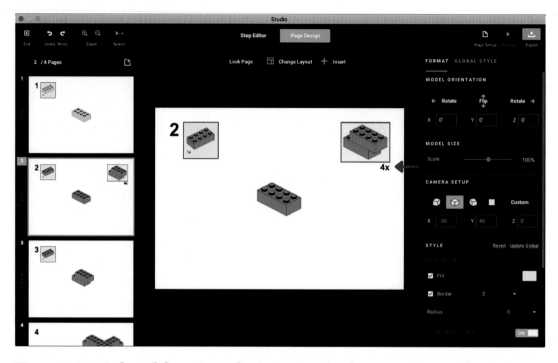

Figure 8-73. *Submodel preview edit options under format section and count multiplier*

You can also edit the background color, turn ON and OFF the count multiplier, and use padding options to change the distance of the submodel preview from its border.

The count multiplier will appear only when you have two or more similar submodels available in one step. As there are four similar submodels present in step 2, that's why the count multiplier is 4, as shown in Figure 8-73.

You can also drag and drop the submodel preview to different corners of the page.

You can also edit the submodel preview under the global style section, as shown in Figure 8-74. You will get all the edit options, except model orientation, model size, and camera setup that you got under the format section. The changes done under the global style section will apply to all other pages.

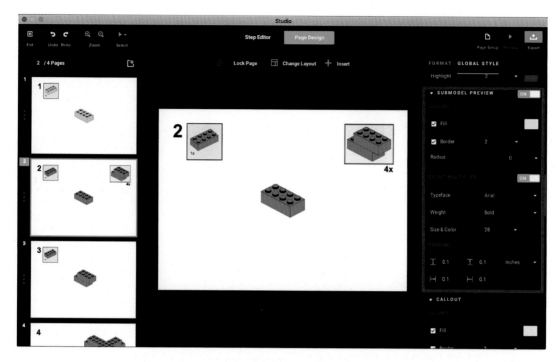

Figure 8-74. *Submodel preview edit options under global style section*

If you turn ON or OFF the submodel preview, it will apply to all the pages. But if you want to turn ON or OFF the submodel preview of any specific page then you can do it under the step view format section, as shown in Figure 8-75.

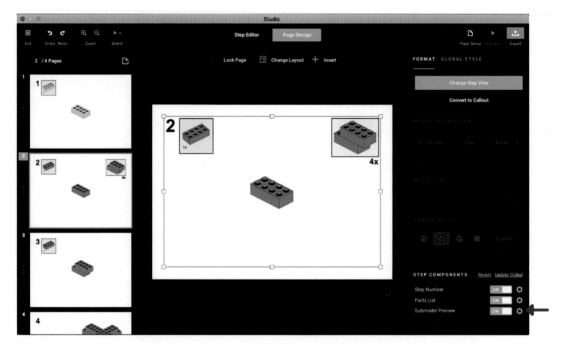

Figure 8-75. *Turn ON or OFF the submodel preview of any specific page*

i. **Callout**

1. The callout is a feature in the Studio that converts the multiple-page submodel steps to a single-box step with the arrow. Callout works best for small submodels with lesser number of parts.

2. When you click the step view section of any submodel steps page, the **convert to callout** button will appear under the format section, as shown in Figure 8-76.

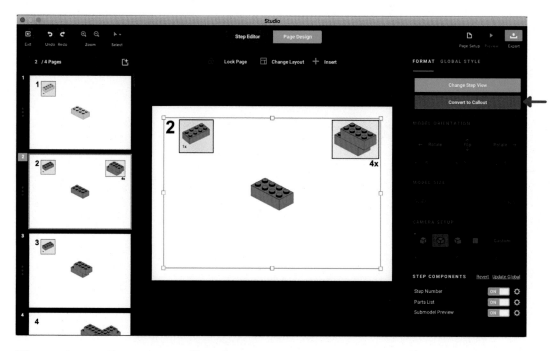

Figure 8-76. *Convert to callout button*

After clicking the convert to callout button, multiple pages of submodel steps will convert into a box with submodel steps, as shown in Figure 8-77. You can change the location of the callout box by dragging and dropping it around the page.

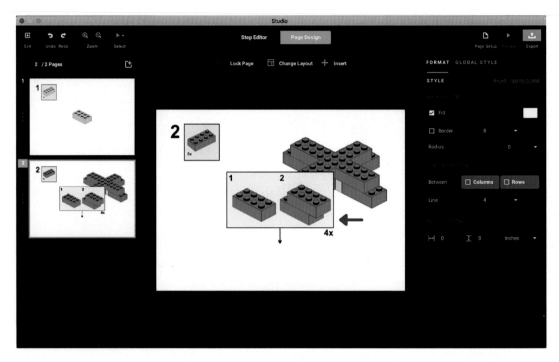

Figure 8-77. *After converting to callout*

When you click on the callout box, the edit options will appear under the format and global style sections, as shown in Figure 8-78. You can change the callout layout, background color, step number, line separator, count multiplier, arrow style, and padding.

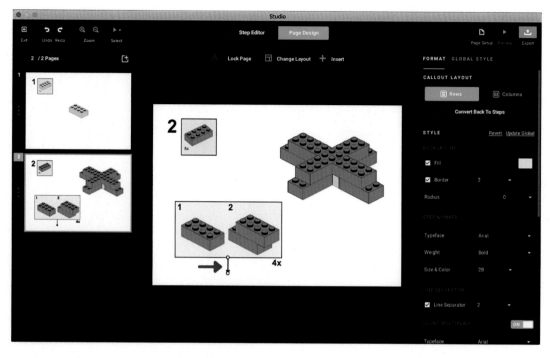

Figure 8-78. *Editing the callout box*

Changes done under the format section will apply only to the selected callout, whereas changes done under the global style will apply to all the callouts.

With the callout box, one arrow will also appear attached to the border, as shown in Figure 8-78. This arrow can be used to show the position of the submodel attached to the main model.

You can drag the arrow head to point it toward the model and you can also change the arrow origin around the callout box border, as shown in Figure 8-78. You can pull multiple arrows from the origin point. The total number of arrows that you can pull out from the arrow origin point depends on the total number of submodels in the selected callout box.

As we have four submodels, we can pull out a maximum of four arrows, and then you can arrange the arrow origin and head based on your requirements, as shown in Figure 8-79.

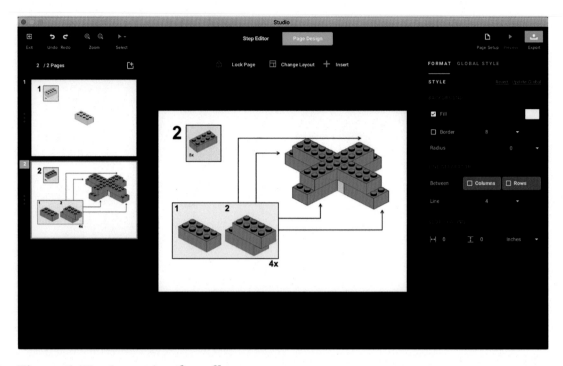

Figure 8-79. *Arranging the callout arrows*

If you need to convert the callout back to the steps mode, first you need to click on the callout box, and then the **convert back to steps** button will appear under the format section, as shown in Figure 8-80. After clicking the button, callout will convert back to steps.

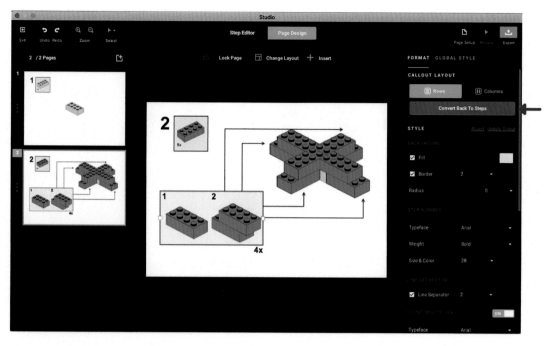

Figure 8-80. *Convert back to steps*

j. **Activate Buffer Exchange**

Activate buffer exchange is a feature in the Studio that helps users to understand where the part is connected in the model by pointing out with an arrow. It is very useful when a part is hidden behind another part.

To activate the buffer exchange, first you need to select the part in the model. I have selected the 1*1 magenta brick, and after that the activate buffer exchange button will appear under the format section, as shown in Figure 8-81.

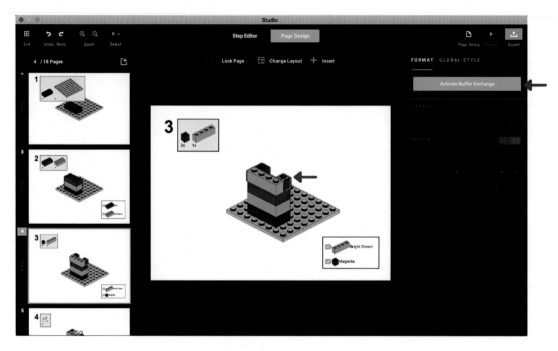

Figure 8-81. *Activate buffer exchange button*

After clicking the **activate buffer exchange** button, three arrows with a small cube will pop up at the center of the selected part and the edit options will appear under the format section, as shown in Figure 8-82.

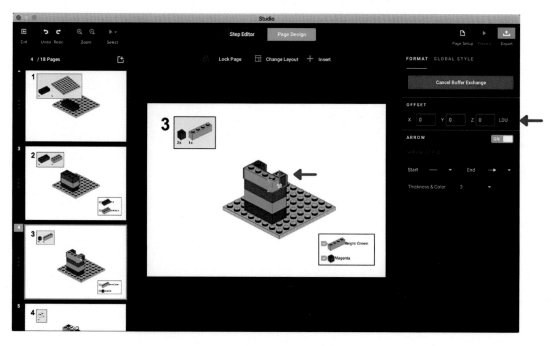

Figure 8-82. *Offset values*

You can use these three arrows attached to the part to move the part in X, Y, and Z directions. You can also change the position of the part by typing the X, Y, and Z values under the offset, as shown in Figure 8-82.

When you shift the 1*1 magenta brick in the Y axis using the arrow attached to it or by typing the Y value under the offset, a black arrow will point out the brick to the origin point, as shown in Figure 8-83. It will help builders to understand the correct location of the part. You can change the arrow style, thickness, and color under the format section.

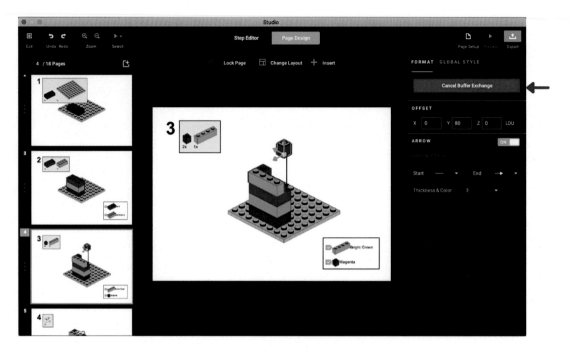

Figure 8-83. *Arrow edit options and cancel buffer exchange*

To go back to normal mode, you need to click on the part to which you activated the buffer exchange and then you need to click the **cancel buffer exchange** button under the format section.

To change the length and direction of the arrow, first you need to click on it and then a small circle will appear at the beginning and end of the arrow, as shown in Figure 8-84. You can drag these circles to change the length and direction.

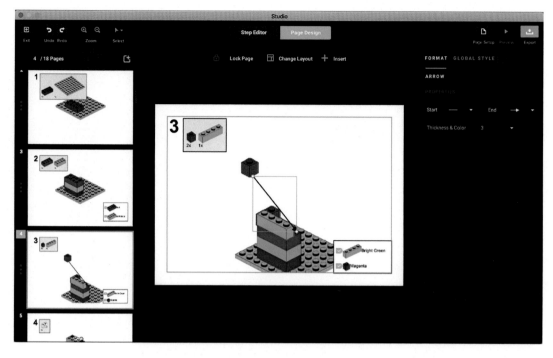

Figure 8-84. *Changing the direction of the arrow*

To bend the arrow, you need to double-click on the arrow from where you want it to bend. After double-clicking, a small circle will appear on the arrow, as shown in Figure 8-85. You can drag this small circle to bend the arrow.

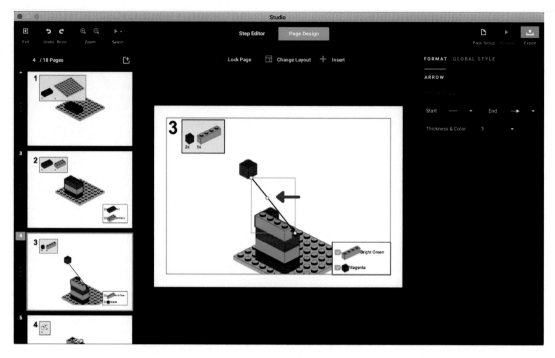

Figure 8-85. *Bending the arrow*

After dragging the small circle between the start and end points of the arrow, it will look as shown in Figure 8-86. You can create multiple bending points on the arrow by double-clicking on the arrow.

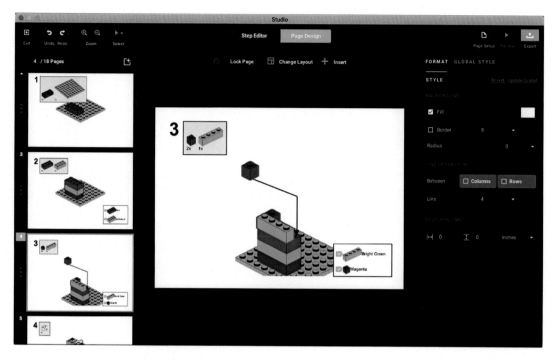

Figure 8-86. *After bending the arrow*

ALIGN TO PREVIOUS STEP IMAGE

To align the current step image to the previous step image, you need to right-click on the step image and select the **align to previous step image** option, as shown in Figure 8-87. The step 4 image will also shift to the right top corner of the page as the step 3 image is also situated in the right top corner, as shown in Figure 8-88.

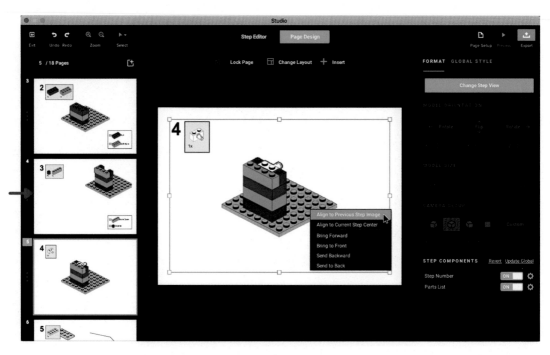

Figure 8-87. *Align to previous step image option*

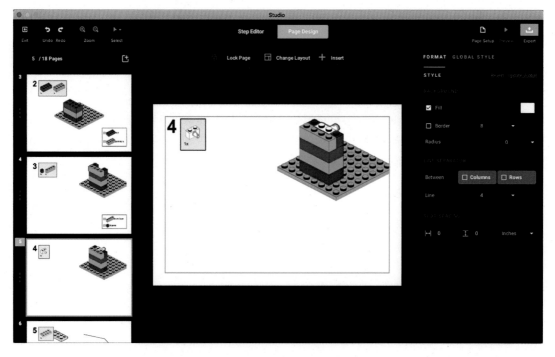

Figure 8-88. *After Aligning to previous step image*

ALIGN TO CURRENT STEP CENTER

To align the current step image to the current step center, you need to right-click on the step image and select the **align to current step center** option, as shown in Figure 8-89. After that, the step 4 image will shift to the center of the page, as shown in Figure 8-90.

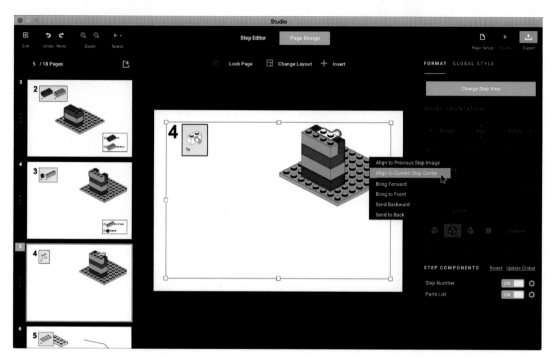

Figure 8-89. *Align to current step center option*

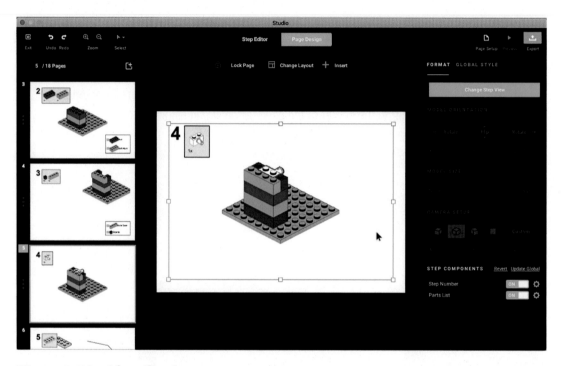

Figure 8-90. *After aligning to current step center*

HIDE AND SHOW THE PAGE NAVIGATOR AND INSPECTOR

To hide the page navigator and inspector, you need to click **view** and select the options as required, as shown in Figure 8-91. After hiding the page navigator and inspector if you wish to unhide them, then again you need to click **view** and select the show navigator and show inspector options, as shown in Figure 8-92.

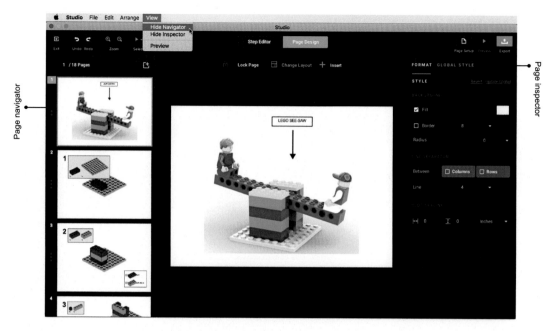

Figure 8-91. *Hide navigator and inspector*

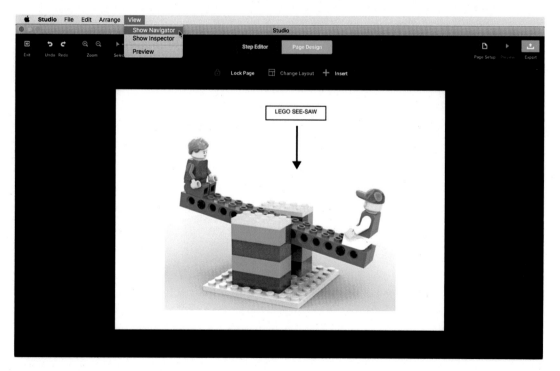

Figure 8-92. *Show navigator and inspector*

- **Page Setup**

When you click on the page setup option situated at the top-right corner of the user interface, the page setup window will open, as shown in Figure 8-93.

Figure 8-93. *Page setup*

You can select the page size from the size drop-down menu as Letter, Legal, Tabloid, A2, A3, A4, or you can customize the size by typing the width and height values. You can also select the size unit, change the page margin, and select the color as RGB or CMYK. Once you finish setting up the page, you can click the apply option, as shown in Figure 8-93.

- **Export**

After setting up the page, you can export your building instructions. When you click the export option situated at the top-right corner of the user interface, the export window will open, as shown in Figure 8-94.

Figure 8-94. *Page export*

You can select the pages, format, size, and file location. After finishing the export settings, you can click the export option at the end of the export window, as shown in Figure 8-94.

After exporting the pages to pdf format, you will get the file, as shown in Figure 8-95.

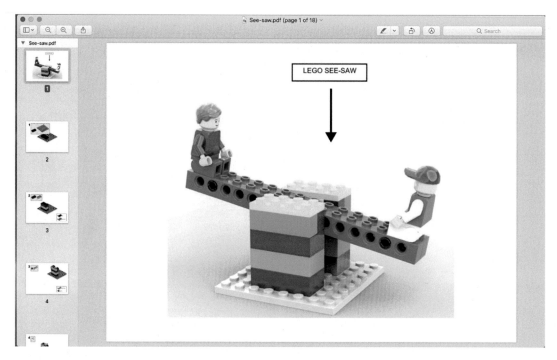

Figure 8-95. *After exporting the pages to pdf*

Mosaic

A mosaic is a picture or art made up of small parts on any surface. You can create your own LEGO mosaic using the mosaic tool available at the top of the Studio user interface, as shown in Figure 8-96.

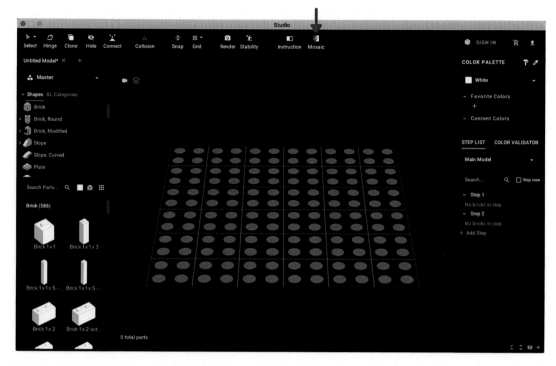

Figure 8-96. *Mosaic tool button*

After clicking the mosaic tool button, a new window will open, as shown in Figure 8-97. You can click the **open new** option to open an image and start creating a brick mosaic art.

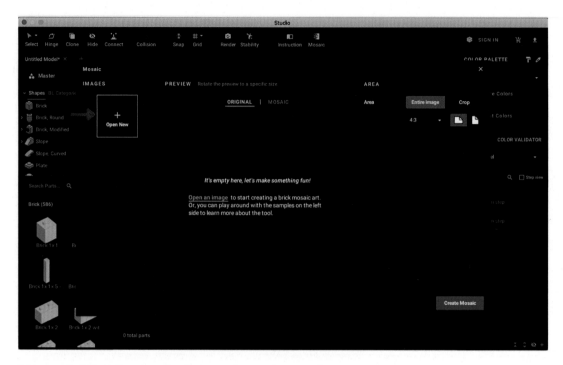

Figure 8-97. *Mosaic window and opening an image*

After opening an image, you can see it in the preview window, as shown in Figure 8-98. You can edit the size of the image under the **area** section. You can keep the entire image for mosaic or crop it. You can also set the crop as landscape or portrait. Once you are satisfied with the image size, you can click the **create mosaic** button present at the bottom right of the mosaic window or click the **mosaic** option in the preview window.

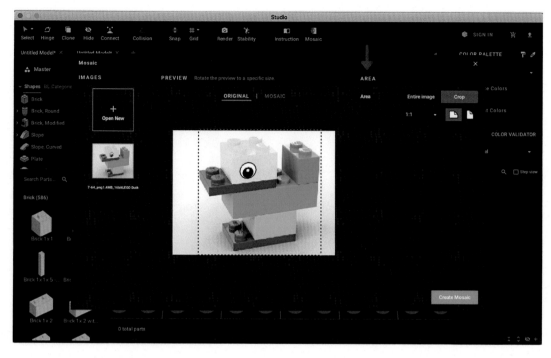

Figure 8-98. *Editing the image*

After clicking the create mosaic button, the image will convert into a brick mosaic in the preview section, as shown in Figure 8-99. You will also find a few setting options for the mosaic on the right side of the preview window. The first setting is the **base size**, as shown in Figure 8-99. You can select the base size based on the studs.

Figure 8-99. *Base size*

The second setting for the brick mosaic is the **base**, as shown in Figure 8-100. If you want to generate a base under your brick mosaic image, turn ON this option. You can also turn on the "use baseplate if possible" option if you want Studio to add a baseplate in the base.

Figure 8-100. *Base and baseplate*

The third setting for the brick mosaic is the **brick type and colors**, as shown in
Figure 8-101. You can select the brick type as plate, tile, brick, round plate, or round tile.
You can also select the color by selecting the option from the color palette drop-down
menu. If you are planning to buy the bricks used in the mosaic from Bricklink, then you
should select the "available bricklink colors" option in the drop-down menu.

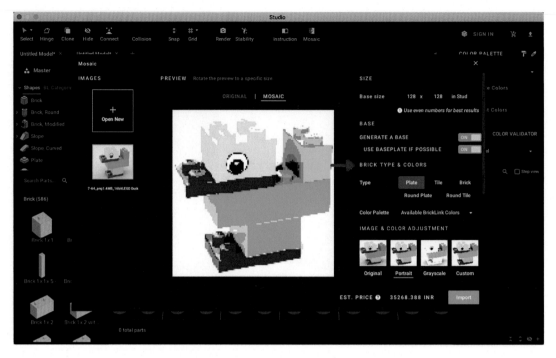

Figure 8-101. *Brick type and color*

The fourth setting for the brick mosaic is the **image & color adjustment**, as shown in Figure 8-102. You can select the image type as original, portrait, greyscale, or custom. When you select the custom option, you will be able to adjust the color manually.

Figure 8-102.   *Image and color adjustment*

The fifth and last setting for the brick mosaic is the **price optimization**, as shown in Figure 8-103. When you turn ON the "use various sized parts" option, the Studio will have more options to choose bricks for your mosaic and the total price of your mosaic will reduce. You can also adjust the color similarity percentage. If you are ready to compromise with the bricks' color, you can reduce the color similarity value and the price will also come down.

Figure 8-103. *Price optimization*

The total price of the mosaic will also vary when you change the base size, brick type, and brick color. Based on your settings, the estimated price of your mosaic will be shown at the end of the mosaic window, as shown in Figure 8-103. If you select generate base option, the base price isn't included in the estimated price. Once you are satisfied with all the settings of your mosaic, you can click the **import** button present at the bottom, as shown in Figure 8-103.

After clicking the **import** button, your mosaic will be imported to the viewport, as shown in Figure 8-104.

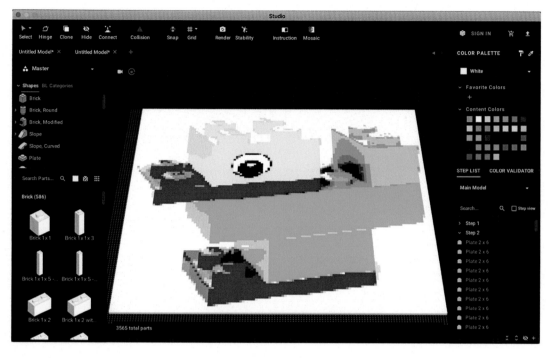

Figure 8-104. *Brick mosaic imported to viewport*

Conclusion

In this chapter, you learned about step editor, page design, and mosaic in detail. You learned different techniques, that is, creating steps for submodel, changing the step number, adding and deleting a step, etc., in the step editor that will help in creating the steps. In the page design, you learned how to create clear and attractive building instructions for your model using insert and page inspector tools. And in the mosaic tool, you learned how to create your own brick mosaic and how to modify the settings to optimize the price.

In the next chapter, you will learn different interesting features of Studio 2.0.

287

CHAPTER 9

Interesting Features of Studio 2.0

In this chapter, you will learn about some interesting features of Studio 2.0 software. After learning these features, you will have a better understanding of the Studio software and you will be able to design and build the model more efficiently.

Preferences

To open the preferences on Mac, you need to click the **Studio** option present at the top left corner and select **preferences**, as shown in Figure 9-1. To open the preferences in Windows you need to click the **Edit** option and select **preferences**.

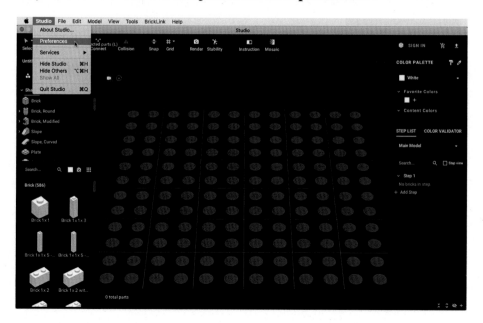

Figure 9-1. *Studio preferences option*

© Vishnu Agarwal 2023
V. Agarwal, *The Art of Virtual LEGO Design*, https://doi.org/10.1007/978-1-4842-8777-4_9

After clicking the preferences option, a new window will open, as shown in Figure 9-2. The preferences setting is divided into three sections: general, appearance, and shortcuts.

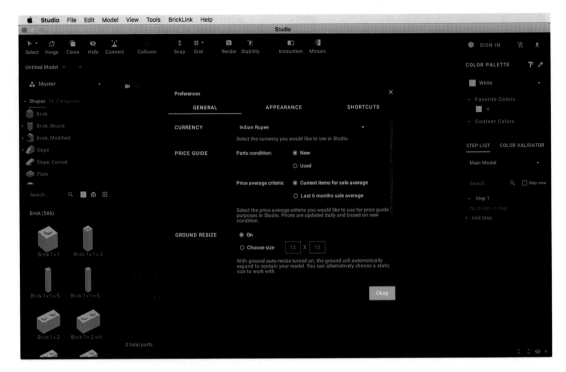

Figure 9-2. *Studio preferences settings*

- **General Preferences**

In the general preferences section, you can select the **currency** of the parts by clicking the currency drop-down menu, as shown in Figure 9-3.

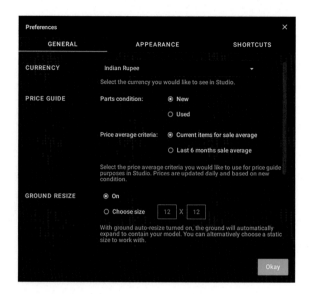

Figure 9-3. *General preferences*

In the **price guide** option, you can select the condition of the parts as new or used and select the price average criteria you would like to use for price guide purposes in Studio, as shown in Figure 9-3. Prices are updated daily and based on new conditions. You can see the price of the parts at the bottom of the viewport as explained in Chapter 5.

If you turn ON the **ground resize** option, the ground will automatically expand to contain your model, and if you choose the static size, the ground size will be fixed, as shown in Figure 9-3.

If you scroll down, you will get more options in the general preferences, as shown in Figure 9-4.

Figure 9-4. *More general preferences*

If you select the check box for **ground elevation**, then if you try to add any part under the ground, the ground will automatically shift under the part. So basically, you won't be able to add a part under the ground. And if you try to delete the base part, the ground elevation will automatically shift to the next available part.

If you select the check box for **brick inserting**, then after placing a part from the bricks palette to the viewport, the part will stick to the mouse pointer and start giving you a copy of the part. I have already explained different ways to place a part from the building palette to the viewport in Chapter 1.

If you select the check box for **auto recovery**, the Studio will recover unsaved models after an unexpected crash. It is a good idea to turn ON this option.

- **Appearance Preferences**

In the appearance preferences section, you can select the **background color** of the viewport by clicking the color box, as shown in Figure 9-5.

Figure 9-5. *Appearance preferences*

You can increase or decrease the **render quality** by moving the slider button, as shown in Figure 9-5. A lower setting will increase performance at the cost of visual quality. A higher setting will improve the visual quality, but requires more computing processing power.

The visual quality of the part is poor with low render quality and good with high render quality in the viewport, as shown in Figures 9-6 and 9-7, respectively. You will get the same result after rendering the part using the rendering tool.

Figure 9-6. *Low render quality*

Figure 9-7. *High render quality*

You can enable and disable the **outline edge** option, as shown in Figure 9-5. When you enable the outline edge option, all the bricks' edges will display with a solid black line in the viewport, as shown in Figure 9-8, and when you disable, there won't be a black outline edge, as shown in Figure 9-9.

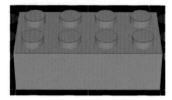

Figure 9-8. *With outline edge*

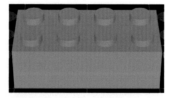

Figure 9-9. *Without outline edge*

You can change the **position of the building palette** to horizontal and vertical by selecting the correct option, as shown in Figure 9-5.

You can enable and disable the **duplex ground** option, as shown in Figure 9-5. If you enable it, the Studio will always show the ground regardless of point of view.

You can also set the frame rate as 30 or 60, as shown in Figure 9-5.

- **Shortcuts Preferences**

In the shortcut preferences section, you can set the **shortcut** keys for brick control, file, edit model, view, bricklink, toolbar, color palette, etc., as shown in Figure 9-10.

Figure 9-10. *Shortcuts preferences*

When you click on the command folders, it will show you all the sub-commands available in it, as shown in Figure 9-11. There are many commands for which shortcut keys are assigned by default. In those predefined shortcuts, a few are locked and a few are open to edit. The locked commands cannot be edited and a lock symbol will be present next to the command name, as shown in Figure 9-11. You can also change the predefined shortcut keys by clicking the shortcut key assigned to the command. After clicking, the shortcut will be highlighted with a green border, as shown in Figure 9-11. After that, you can press the desired key to make that your shortcut.

Figure 9-11. *Shortcuts for brick controls*

There are many commands for which shortcuts have not been assigned by default. If you want to assign a shortcut, click on the commands and press the desired key to make that your shortcut.

If you want to reset all the changes, you need to click the "set to default" option, as shown in Figure 9-11.

Show Recently Used Parts

To open the recently used parts, you need to click view and select the **show recently used parts** option, as shown in Figure 9-12.

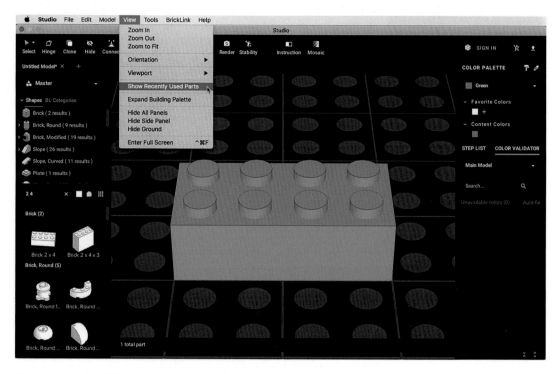

Figure 9-12. *Show recently used parts option*

After that, you can see the recently used parts list on the left side of the Studio user interface, as shown in Figure 9-13. Only two recently used parts will be visible in the list.

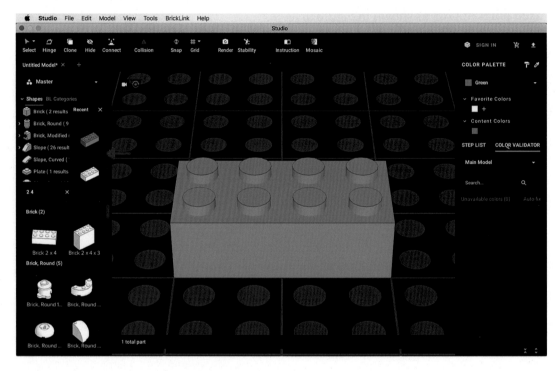

Figure 9-13. *Recently used parts list*

You can move the recently used parts list box by dragging and dropping to different locations in the Studio user interface, and by stretching the sides of the box, you can increase and decrease the size of the box, as shown in Figure 9-14. You can also drag and drop the parts from this list to the viewport.

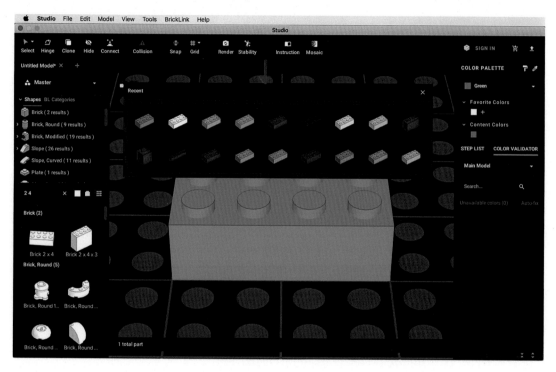

Figure 9-14. *Changing the size of the recently used parts list box*

To hide the recently used parts list, you need to again click view and select **hide the recently used parts option**, or you can click the cross icon on the parts list box, as shown in Figure 9-15.

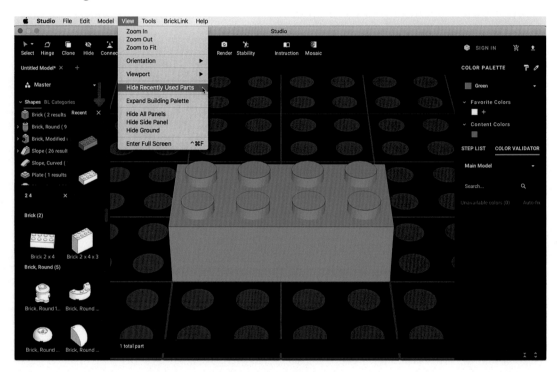

Figure 9-15. *Hiding the recently used parts list*

Expand Building Palette

To expand the building palette, you need to click view and select the **expand building palette** option, as shown in Figure 9-16.

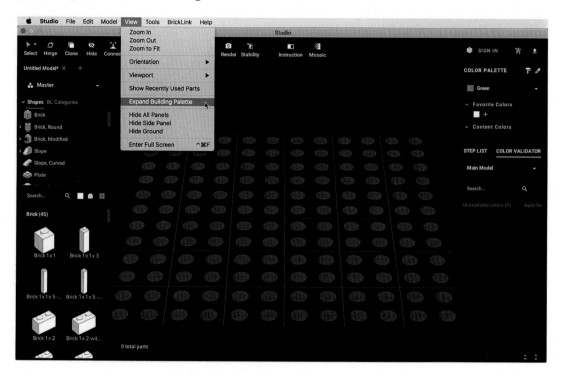

Figure 9-16. *Expand building palette option*

After expanding, the building palette will look as shown in Figure 9-17. In the expanded palette, it is very easy and fast to search any part.

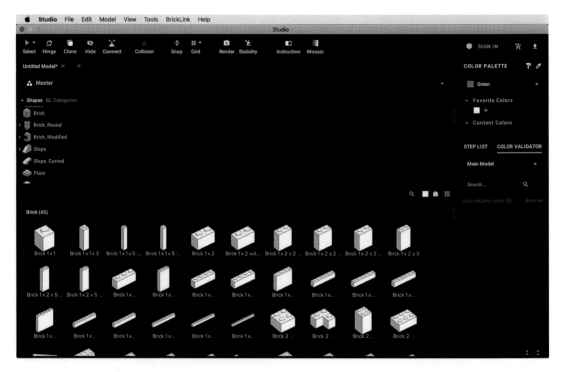

Figure 9-17. *Expanded building palette*

To collapse the building palette, you need to again click view and select the **collapse building palette** option, as shown in Figure 9-18.

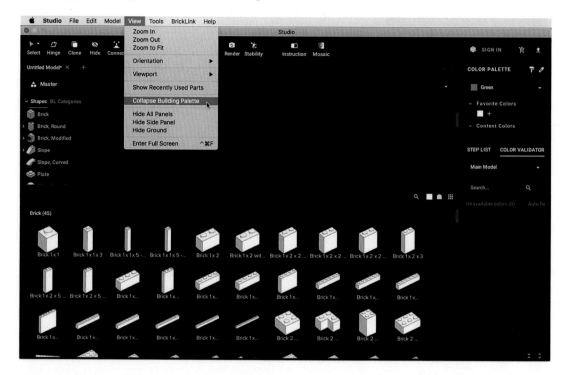

Figure 9-18. *Collapsing building palette*

Hide all Panels, Side Panels, and Ground

To hide the panels and/or ground, you need to click view and select the correct option to hide the panels, hide side panels, and/or hide ground, as shown in Figure 9-19.

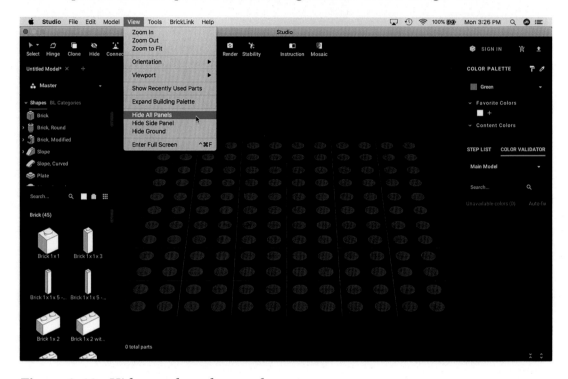

Figure 9-19. *Hide panels and ground*

To unhide the panels and/or ground, you need to again click view and select the correct option to show the panels and/or ground, as shown in Figure 9-20.

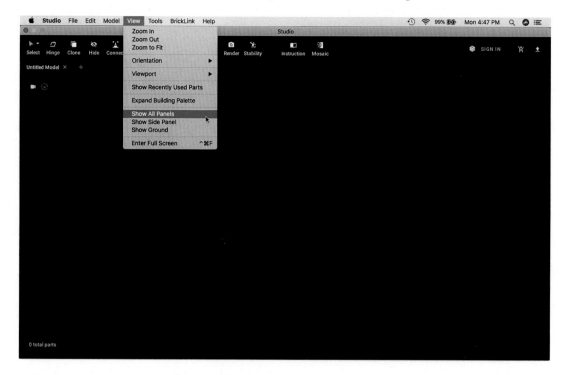

Figure 9-20. *Show panels and ground*

Split and Merge

Split and merge options can be used only for standard bricks and plates. You can divide a brick and plate into smaller bricks and plates using the split option and combine the bricks and plates into a bigger brick and plate using the merge option.

I dragged and dropped a 2*4 brick in the viewport and right-clicked on it. After that, I selected the split option, as shown in Figure 9-21. After splitting, the 2*4 brick is divided into eight 1*1 bricks, as shown in Figure 9-22.

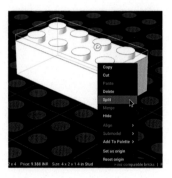

Figure 9-21. *Splitting 2*4 brick*

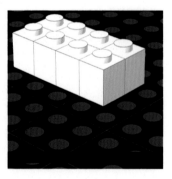

Figure 9-22. *After splitting 2*4 brick*

I selected all the 1*1 bricks, right-clicked on them, and again selected the split option, as shown in Figure 9-23. After splitting, each 1*1 brick is divided into three 1*1 plates, as shown in Figure 9-24.

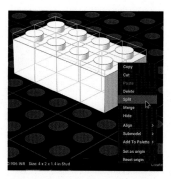

Figure 9-23. *Splitting 1*1 bricks*

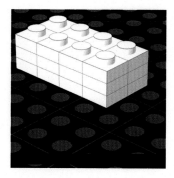

Figure 9-24. *After splitting 1*1 bricks*

To merge the plates, I selected three plates, right-clicked on them, and selected the merge option, as shown in Figure 9-25. After merging, three 1*1 plates converted into a single 1*1 brick, as shown in Figure 9-26.

Figure 9-25. *Merging 1*1 plates*

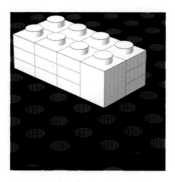

Figure 9-26. *After merging 1*1 plates*

The smallest possible part of a brick is a 1*1 plate. You cannot split a 1*1 plate further. Also, you can only merge those combinations of plates and bricks which are available in real life.

Set as Origin and Reset Origin

By default, the origin is the center of the ground. But if you want to change the origin, then right-click at a point or any part on the ground which you want to make the origin and select the **set as origin** option, as shown in Figure 9-27.

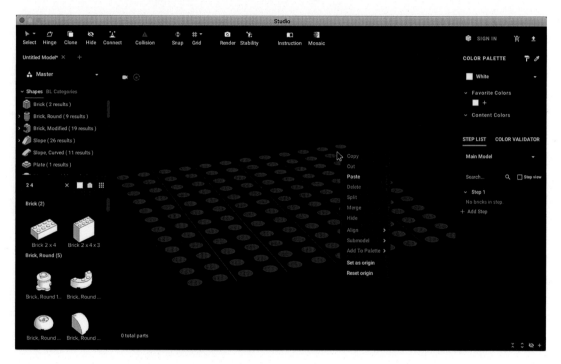

Figure 9-27. *Set as origin option*

After setting the origin, that point of the ground or the part on the ground will shift to the center, as shown in Figure 9-28. Now when you rotate the ground, it will rotate along the new origin.

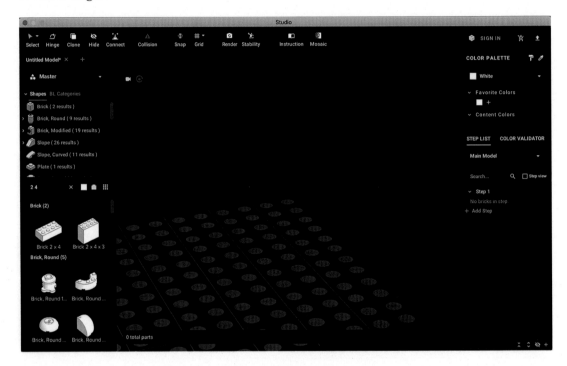

Figure 9-28. *After setting the origin to different location*

To reset the origin back to the center of the ground, you need to right-click on the ground and select the **reset origin** option, as shown in Figure 9-29.

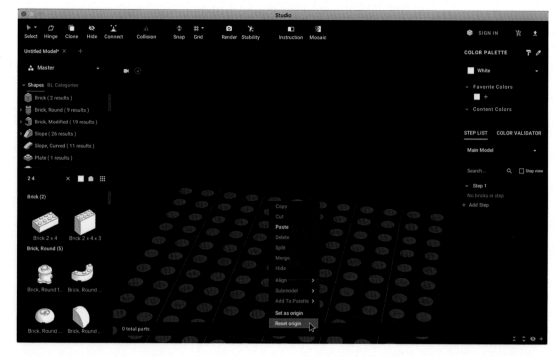

Figure 9-29. *Reset origin*

Sign in to Bricklink

To sign in to bricklink, you need to click the **sign-in** option present at the top right corner of the user interface. After that, a new window will open where you need to type the username and password and click sign-in, as shown in Figure 9-30.

Figure 9-30. *Sign in to bricklink*

If you do not have a bricklink account, visit `www.bricklink.com/` to create your account.

After signing in to bricklink, a **successfully signed into bricklink** window will pop up, as shown in Figure 9-31. You can click **okay** to close this window.

Figure 9-31. *Sign in to bricklink*

To logout from the bricklink account, you need to click the logout button present at the top right corner, as shown in Figure 9-32.

Figure 9-32. *Logout from bricklink*

Model Info

After building a model, if you want to know how many parts you have used in the model, the price of each part, and the size of your model, you need to click on the **model** present at the top of the screen and select the **model info** option, as shown in Figure 9-33.

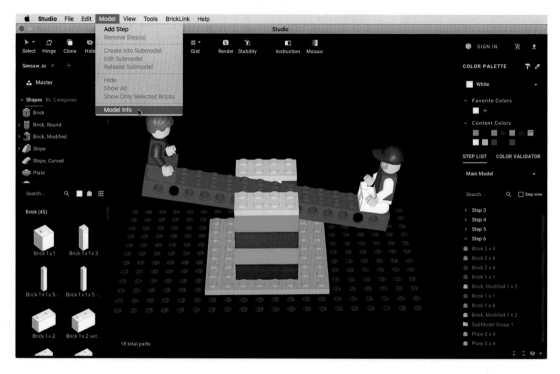

Figure 9-33. *Model info option*

After clicking the model info option, a new window will open which is divided into two sections: parts list and physical information, as shown in Figure 9-34.

Figure 9-34. *Model parts list*

Under the **parts list** section, you will get a model drop-down menu at the top. You can choose to see the parts list of the main model or any submodel. In the parts list, you can see the image, item number, name, color, quantity, and price of the parts, as shown in Figure 9-34. At the bottom of the parts list window, you will also get the total parts and lots used in the model and the total price of the model.

You can also export the parts list in a .csv file by clicking the small arrow present next to the model drop-down menu, as shown in Figure 9-34.

Under the **physical information** section also, you will get a model drop-down menu at the top. You can choose to see the physical information of the main model or any submodel. After selecting the model, you can see the width, length, and height of the model in studs, inches, and centimeters. You can also see the weight of the model in ounces and grams, as shown in Figure 9-35.

Figure 9-35. *Model physical information*

Add to Wanted List

Once you finish designing your model in Studio, you can add the parts of your model to the wanted list and order from bricklink. To add the parts to the wanted list you must be logged in to bricklink. After that, to add the parts to the wanted list you can click the **shopping cart icon** at the top right corner of the user interface or click the **add to wanted list** option in the model information window, as shown in Figure 9-36.

Figure 9-36. *Add to wanted list option*

After clicking the "add to wanted list," the "upload to wanted list" bricklink page will open in your default browser, as shown in Figure 9-37. You can also upload a wanted list file from your computer. You can assign a name to your uploaded wanted list and click **proceed to verify items**, as shown in Figure 9-37.

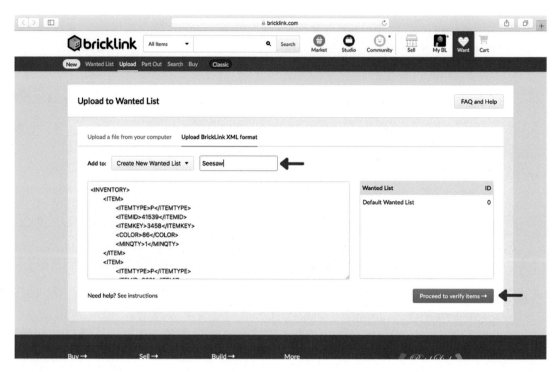

Figure 9-37. *Upload to wanted list*

After clicking the "proceed to verify items," it will take you to the next page where you can verify the parts condition, price, quantity, etc., as shown in Figure 9-38. When you scroll down, you will get the option to "add to wanted list," as shown in Figure 9-39.

Figure 9-38. *Verify and add items to your wanted list*

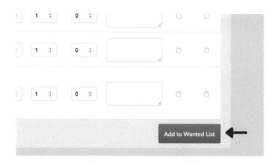

Figure 9-39. Add to wanted list

After clicking the "add to wanted list," items will be successfully added to the wanted list, and a successfully added message will be displayed, as shown in Figure 9-40. When you click the **View seesaw** option, as shown in Figure 9-40, you can see the wanted list on the next page and select a few items or click the **buy all** option to buy the parts, as shown in Figure 9-41.

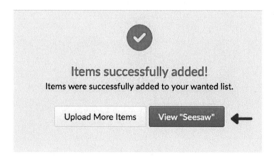

Figure 9-40. "Wanted list successfully added" message

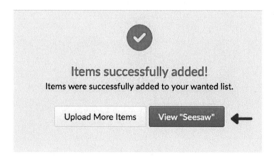

Figure 9-41. Buy the parts from wanted list

Upload to My Studio

If you want to share your creations with the world, you can upload your model to **My Studio** on bricklink. To upload to "My Studio," you must be logged in to bricklink. You need to click the arrow icon facing upward at the top right corner of the Studio user interface, as shown in Figure 9-42.

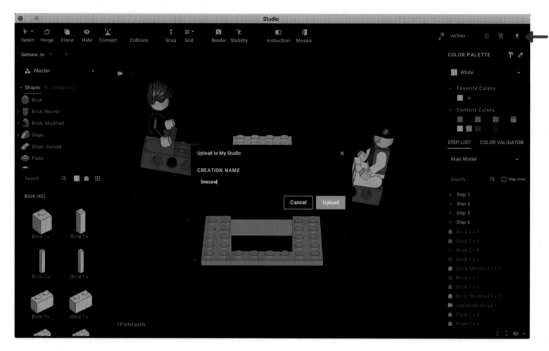

Figure 9-42. *Creation name*

After clicking the "upload to My Studio" icon, a new window will pop up where you can type the name of your creation, as shown in Figure 9-42. After writing the name and clicking "upload," another window will pop up saying that "your model was successfully uploaded to My Studio," as shown in Figure 9-43.

Figure 9-43. *View "My Studio"*

You can click "View My Studio" to open your design on bricklink. You can talk about the background of your design, techniques used, etc. You can also embed pictures or videos.

Build Together

If you want to work on the same model simultaneously with your friend, you can use the **Build Together** feature. To activate this feature, you need to click the bricklink option present at the top of the screen and select the **Build Together** option, as shown in Figure 9-44. To use the Build Together feature, you must be logged in to bricklink.

Figure 9-44. *Build Together option*

After clicking the Build Together option, a new window will pop up at the center of the screen, as shown in Figure 9-45. You can host the session or join an already existing host. When you click on the **host** section, your id and port will be displayed. You can also set the password for your session, which is optional. After that, you can click the **host button** at the bottom of the Build Together window, as shown in Figure 9-45.

Figure 9-45. *Build Together host settings*

After clicking the host button, your session will be live and the success notification window will pop up, as shown in Figure 9-46. Once the session has been created, friends can join you using your ID and the session password.

Figure 9-46. *Host success notification*

Once the session is live, a chat icon will appear on the left side of the user interface. Once you click that icon, a chat window will open, as shown in Figure 9-47. You can drag and drop the chat window to different locations on the screen.

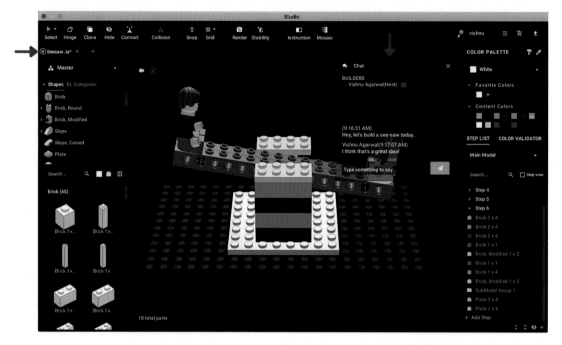

Figure 9-47. *Build together session user interface*

When the session is live, you will see a **green wired plug** icon in the project name, as shown in Figure 9-47. Once you disconnect the session this icon will also disappear.

To disconnect the Build Together feature, again you need to click the bricklink option present at the top of the screen and select the **Build Together** option, as shown in Figure 9-48. After that, a new window will pop up for the reconfirmation of the disconnecting, as shown in Figure 9-49. You can click on the **disconnect button** to stop the session. Also, make sure to save your work if you would like to keep any progress made from the Build Together session.

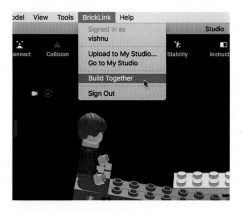

Figure 9-48. *Build together option to disconnect*

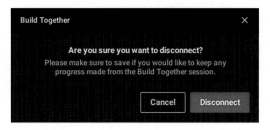

Figure 9-49. *Disconnect build together*

To join an already existing host, you need to click the **join** section and use the host ID and password to join the session, as shown in Figure 9-50. After clicking the join button, a **join success notification** window will pop up, as shown in Figure 9-51.

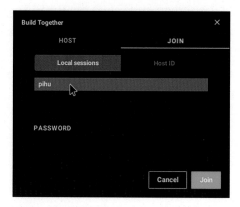

Figure 9-50. *Build Together join settings*

Figure 9-51. *Join success notification*

The viewport is independent of each other. If you rotate, pan, and zoom in or out the camera, it will not be visible to others. But if you do any changes in the model, it will be visible to the host and other members in the session. After joining a session, you can also save the host's project to your system.

Conclusion

In this chapter, you learned about different interesting features of Studio, that is, selecting the currency of the part, render quality, shortcuts, splitting and merging bricks, build together, and many more. All these features will help you to increase your speed of building a model in Studio.

Index

A

Animation features, Studio 2.0
    background color, 170
    camera center, 174–176
    camera setup
        camera rotation, 172
        field of view, 174
        pan, 173
        zoom scale, 174
    effects, 167, 168
    light source
        rotation, 171
        type and position, 170, 171
    material effects
        scratches, 178, 179
        stud logo, 176, 177
        UV degradation, 177, 178
    quality, 166, 167
    render quality, 169

B

Bitmap Image File (BMP), 181
.bmp image format, 182
BrickLink categories, 50, 51
Building palette, 5, 6, 37–57, 301–303
Building sequence effect, 168
Building tools of Studio 2.0, 13
    Clone tool, 24, 25
    collision tool, 28, 29
    connect tool, 27, 28
    Hide tool, 25, 26
    Hinge tool, 17–22
    manual mode, 22–24
    select tool, 13–16
    snap option, 30, 32, 33
    Snap tool (*see* Snap tool)
Build together session user
    interface, 324
Buy all option, 319
By Color select tool, 14
By Connected select tool, 16
By Type and color select tool, 15
By Type select tool, 15

C

Callout, 260–265
Callout arrows, 261–264
Callout box, 261–264
Camera pan, 155, 173
Chrome colors, 66, 67
Clone tool, 24–25, 96
Clutch power issues, 187, 188
Coarse grid, 31, 32
Collision tool, 28, 29
Color palette, 59, 78, 79
    change part color, 64, 65
    color by shade type, 74, 75
    colors list, 65–74
    content colors, 78, 79
    favorite color, 77, 78
    Grab color from part option, 63, 64
    hide unavailable colors, 75–77
    paint, selected color option, 59–62

Printed in the United States
by Baker & Taylor Publisher Services